WOMEN IN TECH

TAKE YOUR CAREER TO THE NEXT LEVEL

with Practical Advice and Inspiring Stories

TARAH WHEELER VAN VLACK

Foreword by Esther Dyson

CONTRIBUTORS: Angie Chang / Katie Cunningham
Keren Elazari / Miah Johnson / Kristin Toth Smith
Kamilah Taylor / Brianna Wu

SASQUATCH BOOKS
SEATTLE

Printed in the United States of America

Published by Sasquatch Books
20 19 18 17 16   9 8 7 6 5 4 3 2 1

Editor: Hannah Elnan
Production editor: Emma Reh:
Design: Anna Goldstein
Puzzles: Mike Selinker, Gaby Weidling, and Ryan "LostboY" Clarke
Copyeditor: Janice Lee

Library of Congress Cataloging-in-Publication Data is available.

ISBN: 978-1-63217-066-8

Sasquatch Books
1904 Third Avenue, Suite 710
Seattle, WA 98101
(206) 467-4300
www.sasquatchbooks.com
custserv@sasquatchbooks.com

Foreword © Esther Dyson
The Crusader © Angie Chang
The Developer © Kamilah Taylor
The Hacker © Keren Elazari
The Educator © Kristin Smith
The Parent © Katie Cunningham
The Gamer © Brianna Wu
The Sysadmin © Miah Johnson

Certified Chain of Custody
SUSTAINABLE Promoting Sustainable Forestry
FORESTRY
INITIATIVE www.sfiprogram.org
SFI-01268

SFI label applies to the text stock

‹WOMEN IN TECH›

```python
#!/usr/bin/env python3
"""Bernoulli numbers according to Ada Lovelace.
Note that Ada's numbering is off by one compared to modern numbering;
AB[n] == B[n+1].
Shamelessly stolen from https://gist.github.com/terotil/
3f83a473f372d31f55d5
"""


from fractions import Fraction

memo = {}

def ab(n):
    if n in memo:
        return memo[n]
    assert isinstance(n, int) and n > 0, n
    if n%2 == 0:
        return Fraction()
    nterms = (n-1) // 2
    arg = nterms + 1
    sum = Fraction(-1, 2) * Fraction(2*arg - 1, 2*arg + 1)
    for i in range(nterms):
        degree = 2*i + 1
        v = term(degree, arg)
        sum += ab(degree) * v
    res = -sum
    memo[n] = res
    return res

def term(degree, n):
    num = 1
    den = 1
    for i in range(degree):
        num *= 2*n - i
        den *= 2 + i
    return Fraction(num, den)

cipher = {}
for b in [65, 97]:
    for i in range(26):
        cipher[b+i] = b + (i+13)%26

def caesar(s):
    return s.translate(cipher)

def main():
    for n in range(1, 37):
        a = ab(n)
        print("AB[%2s] == %21s / %s" % (n, a.numerator, a.denominator))
    print(caesar("uggcf://jjj.sbhezvyno.pu/onoontr/fxrgpu.ugzy"))

if __name__ == '__main__':
    main()
```

Creating this book took the entire tech community. Without you all, I would never have had the audacity to even attempt it. The power of just one outspoken person can change the world—Now, imagine an orchestra, joyful and riotous. I hear your music, and to you all I offer this dedication.

\<CONTENTS\>

<FOREWORD>

As you read this book, you'll bring to it your own goals and history. And that's the point. Women are not all alike; your challenge in life is not to live as a woman, but to live as your own unique self. So in this foreword, I speak only for myself. I feel comfortable with the culture of technology and science, and I try to think logically and rationally. I've been part of the tech community since the 1970s. I got into it because it was the most interesting thing happening at the time. I studied economics in college, and took a job as a fact-checker for *Forbes*—then an investors' magazine—shortly after graduating. I loved researching tech businesses; they had not just the financial prospects but also the social and intellectual elements to keep me interested: artificial intelligence, online communications (the Internet was not yet a thing, and I worked on a manual typewriter and got press releases by fax). Almost forty years later, with new technologies still emerging, I'm still watching with fascination. And I'm still learning, as the active founder of a nonprofit startup focused on health.

If I can tell you anything, it's this: Find your own success. Don't let your mother or boyfriend or colleagues define it for you. Try to create your own job. If you want to found companies, do that. I haven't worked for anyone since I was thirty-something. That may not be your thing. The challenge is how to go from where you are to where you want to be, not where someone else wants you to be.

You always have an alternative. I'm happy doing what I love. You have to see the whole spectrum of what's available to you. I was fired at *Forbes*, and it wasn't the end of my life. I'm still here. You're the actor running your own life through a script you write, not an automaton helplessly following its program. Don't choose the script that limits you. I had a lot of wonderful choices, but I know a lot of people who didn't and don't. Bad things may happen, but you can still decide how to deal with them. There's help out there for you, and a lot of it is in this book.

Everything sounds easy in theory. Have an idea, form a company, sell it five years later, and retire. In practice, it's much more complicated than that. People don't understand how complex life, tech, and business are, and they focus more on a job title instead of what they want to do. The bravery of the women writing in this book and sharing their lives with you is inspiring. They're showing you from the inside what it's really like to make the best choice possible in impossible situations. You're not defined by what other people think you are, or what you used to be. You are defined by your actions. Hear the advice and stories here, make your own choices, accept the consequences, and live your own life.

—ESTHER DYSON

\<INTRODUCTION\>

Tech. It's a scary word to a lot of people. It describes a field of endeavor, a career, a style of thinking, and our goals for the future. In the 1400s, the forefront of human thought was alchemy and astronomy. In the 1500s, the place to be was natural philosophy. In the 1600s, mathematics. In the 1700s, political science. The most creative people are drawn to the field of human endeavor in which the biggest advances are being made. Now tech is the place to be.

So why does it seem as if women, who make up 51 percent of the world's population, just can't manage to break into the most exciting field of human endeavor on the planet today?

I have a very scary statistic for you. The number of women working in computer science and achieving computer science degrees achieved its height thirty-one years ago. In 1984, 38 percent of computer science degrees were awarded to women. In 2014, less than 10 percent were. No matter how many role models, mentors, and larger-than-life superheroines exist in popular media, we are failing. We are failing to bring women into technology in the first place, and the number of women in technology is dropping every year.

There are a number of potential reasons why women and technology don't seem to mix. I've heard people talk about sexism, discrimination, biological imperatives, evolutionary and social preferences, and a host of other reasons why women just don't seem to be a "good fit" in the technological field.

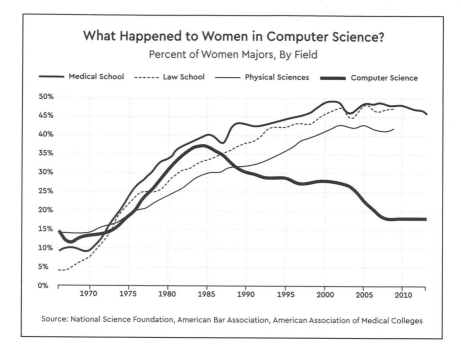

What Happened to Women in Computer Science?
Percent of Women Majors, By Field

——— Medical School ------ Law School ——— Physical Sciences ▬▬ Computer Science

Source: National Science Foundation, American Bar Association, American Association of Medical Colleges

You know what? I don't give a damn why someone else thinks I don't belong. I love technology, and I feel joy every single day that I get to invent something new, bring people a new perspective, invent a new automated process that gives time back to someone else, or make the world a better place. I realize that technology can seem like a field that just doesn't have a place for women, and I want to do something to change that.

It turns out that the reason we just don't think women would be a good fit in technology is unconscious social bias, not any kind of conspiracy. Screaming at men for being sexist doesn't lead to anything except for defensiveness and counterattacks. Most men in tech are just people interested in creating a great life for themselves and are willing to help others if they're given a plan—and not blamed for everything wrong in the world.

The best way to combat unconscious social bias is to bring it out into the open and see all the ways in which women not only can but *should* be part of technology.

I really like men. I dig them just fine. Most of my friends are men. I married a particularly spectacular example of the gender. I generally tend to get along better with men. I don't know if that's because of the way I've been socially conditioned or if it's just the way I'm built, but I frequently find myself in the position of translating one gender to another in technology. The thing I have found to be the most effective in changing people's minds and hearts is telling stories. Often, I relay the stories of women I know who've been successful and let people draw their own conclusions. Real empathy is the only true answer to the women in technology problem.

Wouldn't it be wonderful if six-year-old girls, thirteen-year-old girls, thirty-three-year-old girls, and seventy-two-year-old girls all realized that they had a place and a purpose in the most exciting field of exploration right now? I want to build space robots. I want to develop a way for people who've never spoken the same language to chat with each other from ten thousand miles away and experience translation in real time. I think that if I want public information and it's not readily available to me, I can and should find a way to make it accessible via the Internet. I think that I should be able to play beautiful, innovative, and imaginative games that have protagonists to whom I can relate. For that to happen, we need diverse voices in technology. The old model of just hiring your friends and buddies has led to a critical shortage of unique points of view.

It's time to change this depressing statistic. It's time to buck the trend. In this book, in addition to giving you advice on some simple ways to forge your own path in your tech career, I'm going to share the autobiographies of seven amazing women in seven different fields of technology. You'll find out what it's like to have children while working a high-pressure programming job. You'll learn what it's like to be a cyberwarrior in Israel. You'll learn what it's like to emigrate from Jamaica as a technologist. You'll learn what it's like to transition to a different gender while trying to keep your servers from transitioning to a defunct state. You'll even find out what it's like to be driven from your home for standing up for the right of women game developers to tell the stories they want to tell. These women are actual technologists; every single person in this book is a developer, architect, programmer, or hacker. They're not going to offer you any advice. They're just going to tell you who they are, why they made the choices they did, and why they love technology so much.

You will come away from this book with a deep understanding of the different perspectives of women in tech, as well as their goals and their reasons for going into the field. You'll learn how you can create the best possible tech career for yourself while acknowledging the discrimination and sexism rampant in the industry. Finally, you'll know better than ever before why it is that you should (or shouldn't) go into tech.

I promise you this: by the time you're done reading this book, you will know what it's like to be a woman in technology. You should be able to do what you choose with your life, and you shouldn't close off technology as a potential field for your career because you're afraid of the stories you've heard about how hostile the environment is to women. Technology is not a monolithic field full of jackasses. Well, it is, in fact, liberally sprinkled with jackasses, but that's true of just about any field. Mostly, technology is full of weird, misunderstood, somewhat awkward, and generally well-meaning human beings. If you've ever felt as if you don't belong, chances are you're going to find plenty of friends in tech who know just how you feel. We are the weird ones. We're the ones who stayed after school and did extra homework. We are the ones who programmed in Fortran while sporting mohawks. We're the ones who had no patience for being told "this is how it's always been done." We're the ones who knew there was a better way to do it. We are the ones who ignored the rules and made up our own. We are the ones who know what it's like to be an outsider. We think you should join us.

Maybe you think that you had to start programming computers at the age of five to be able to get a computer science degree and go work for a big tech company. Maybe you think you're not smart enough. Maybe you think you just won't fit in. Well, you're right about not fitting in. None of us fit in anywhere. I can tell you this, though: only two people in this entire book have computer science degrees. I didn't start programming until I was twenty-three. I had built some computers before that, and I had been around them for some time, but the thought that I could be a technologist never even entered my mind while I was young. I started as a human communications major and ended up in complex systems and political science. Still, I've been a scientist and a systems engineer my entire life—even when I didn't know the words for these things. For more than a decade I've been working in technology in one way or another, and there is nothing to stop you from joining the technological field at any age and with any degree or none at all. Nothing irritates me more than hearing women tell me, "Oh, I could never do what you do. I'm just not smart enough." Let me assure you that, in fact, there are smart people in tech, dull people in tech, and everyone in between. I've been in academia, and I've seen a lot of very, very stupid physicists succeed just fine in getting doctorates and tenure. The only thing that matters is whether or not you want to be a technologist. If you do, I will do my best to help you get there.

The secret to being in technology is simple: find the thing you love and never let it go. If you love programming or making websites or developing new technology or building robots or soldering boards or being a hacker, just keep doing it, and we will help you find a way to make money at it.

I'm nothing special when it comes to being a computer programmer. The difference between me and someone who's been a programmer for dozens of years is that I came in through the side door. I started with an outsider's view of the field and then worked my way in. I have a passion for building and understanding systems. I've been collecting data on interviewing and tech careers for years, and I can tell you that the view from outside helped me and will now help you to understand how you can succeed in tech. This perspective is what's helped me coach hundreds of women to get the jobs they want. It's what lets me see the difference between a woman's experience and a man's experience in tech interviews. I run workshops, speak publicly, and teach extensively on all the ways that women can both be themselves and figure out how to make tech work as a career field. I'm no self-help guru. I'm just a hacker. I don't have a lot of patience for rules and people who tell me I can't do something I want to do. If you're someone who has a just-can't-quit attitude, then I think we're going to get along just fine.

Here's what moved me to write this book: no one else has. As far as I'm concerned, that's a good enough reason to do just about anything. I know there are women who are smarter than I am, and I know for a fact there are lots of better developers out there. I also know this: I care enough to spend years of my life trying to help bridge this gap between women and the careers they deserve to have. It is a shame and a crime to see half the potential technical talent in the world go to waste. I think I can help in some small way, and this book is my answer to not having had any of this advice when I started out. I'm trying to leave the world a better and more creative place than I found it, and I refuse to believe that women shouldn't be in technology because somehow they are biologically not suited for it. I refuse to believe that I am not as creative or as capable as my esteemed male colleagues. I believe that you should refuse to accept limitations that other people try to impose on you. I believe mentorship is the only real way to learn what you need to know in tech.

I learn a great deal from my mentors and in turn teach my mentees. It's going to become your responsibility to mentor others based on what you learned from reading this book and your own experience in technology. The act of giving what you know to someone else helps you grow ever more confident in your own career, and it does even more good for you than them. Mentoring is not optional. You will teach others who and what you are whether you like it or not. Do so mindfully, and remember you're always setting an example for someone.

You'll find it most helpful to read this book cover to cover, as opposed to à la carte. I have organized my advice and my stories, as well as the stories of my contributing authors, not as a textbook but as a journey through a technical career. We'll go through the lessons I've learned and discuss how you can apply them, and hear stories from my amazing contributors right at the moment when I wish I could have heard them during my career. I can't wait to share this knowledge with you! Let's get started.

Hello world. These remarkable women would love you to break their codes.

THE SCIENTIST
Tarah Wheeler Van Vlack

To her credit, Mom always did her best to answer my perpetual "why" questions instead of saying "because I said so." Most importantly, she and my dad taught me how to find the answers to my own questions. I was homeschooled on a little farm in Silverton, Oregon, by two ex-army spies (turned preacher and homemaker). I had a hell of a Socratic education. "Today is entomology. Go find a bug you never noticed before and write a report on it, including its Latin name. Write a short story about why it's here on the farm." Now that's the way to get a kid to love school. Also, bugs are cool.

We didn't have much money, so we often did side work as a family, like flipping cars, berry picking, and selling mistletoe Mom shot out of oak trees (those army skills did come in handy). One summer, when I was eight, I wanted money to buy a bike. I started by picking blueberries in the fields of the Willamette Valley. Dad said, "Here's your first lesson in business." Instead of selling berries back to the farmer at $0.25 a pound (a good picker could pick a pound every minute or two, and this was when the minimum wage was around $3.10 per hour), I bought twenty pounds of blueberries I picked for $0.50 a pound. Then we went door to door selling those same blueberries for $2.00 a pint. I had a bike in a week.

The funny thing is that while Mom taught me math, Spanish, grammar, and how to clean just about anything (that last is less a subject and more a state of existence) and Dad taught me classical

Greek, German, and philosophy, for my literary education, they just turned me loose on books they hadn't read. Do not feed a seven-year-old Spenser and the Brontë sisters and a nine-year-old *The Decameron* and Chaucer unless you want to end up with a seriously weird eleven-year-old reading Dante, Stoker, and D. H. Lawrence books with extremely sober jacket designs. Mom just told me to start at one end of the Great Books of the Western World and keep going, bless her mathematically inclined heart.

I was still quite naive about a great number of things, mostly to do with other people. I was a very introverted child—not shy but introverted. It was exhausting figuring out what I was supposed to say to other children, and I always seemed to pick the wrong option in the decision tree. I spent a lot of time alone. On our horse farm in the 1980s, there wasn't much to fear, and I'd often finish my chores, be done with my schoolwork in a few minutes, and have the rest of the day to trail-ride. As long as I was back by the dinner bell and told Mom if I'd be out past a few miles, I didn't get in trouble. I could ride out all day into the forest and surrounding fields and farms.

I don't know if my thoroughly idyllic childhood is possible anymore. Even now, introverted children are often treated as mentally ill or antisocial, and while Mom did her best to get me around other children (I was that kid over in the corner with my nose in a book), I actually had most of the solitude I needed. Though Mom and Dad are both extroverts, they had the good sense to see that I was happy and learning, and left me alone almost as much as I would have liked.

Here's what all that alone time did to me: I realized from maybe six years old on that nothing was going to happen or change unless I personally did it. If I didn't bring splints out on the trail, I wouldn't be able to set my fingers (one breaks a lot of fingers and toes around horses, mostly fractures or crushing injuries). If I didn't bring a canteen or find clean groundwater, I'd be mighty thirsty by end of day. If I didn't break trail and cut down blackberries, there would be no trail there when I came back. That should help illuminate what came later: a preference for solitude, a need and an ability to find out why, and a willingness to break trail without needing anyone's bloody permission is probably what makes me "me." Also possibly my hypercompetitiveness. It wasn't OK for girls to be as competitive and ambitious as I was. I competed in horse shows and 4-H, and I was constantly told to be softer, quieter, less aggressive, and nicer. After all, I was a rodeo princess, and they're supposed to be compliant, precious, and sugary sweet. Fortunately, stubbornness is another of my character traits. I like to win. A lot.

All good things, as Captain Picard might say. When I was twelve, I was injured badly by a lovely but skittish palomino quarter horse; she rolled over me in a serious accident. I spent months in bed and learned that year to absolutely despise daytime television. I still hear music from *The Price Is Right* in my nightmares. I was no longer able to help on the farm, and we were always very close to the line. Without my doing farm chores and helping with odd jobs (and with no need to keep horses anymore), we had to move off the farm.

When my family moved closer to Portland, I was thirteen, and I tried public school for the first time. I was an innocent dreamer in just about every way, and I did not make an auspicious debut. I wanted to be left alone, which is the one thing that does not happen in public junior high. Also, you're apparently not supposed to challenge authority. Remember that short story "The Most Dangerous Game"? Some less-than-perspicacious school official had put me in normal English instead of the advanced class, and our first assignment was to write the missing fight scene. As a disciple of the Dumas and Bulwer-Lytton school of florid prose, I inserted lots of flashing swords, ripped tapestries, and at one point, a vase "arcing" across the room. That word came back marked as misspelled; the teacher inserted a *k* into it. I raised my hand and told the teacher she'd marked my paper incorrectly, and she told me to shut my mouth. I told her to get a dictionary. She threw me out of her class, and I don't mean politely at the end; I was booted out to sit in the hall. I was in advanced English a day later, away from that kind of corseted thinking. Challenging authority is cool.

Take a guess as to what happens to strange thirteen-year-old girls who act like that in junior high. Now they call it vicious bullying, beating, sexual assault, and in some cases actual torture, but back then I was just told to toughen up and laugh it off. Bullying like that doesn't toughen you up; it breaks you. I was broken for a while. I spent a lot of time in the library playing Oregon Trail whenever teachers would let me out of class. There was a librarian there, so not too much could happen to me. I started forensics (speech and debate) in high school, and though I found my clan of speech geeks, as we were called, I was exhausted and had whatever the high school equivalent of combat fatigue would be called. At the same time, my family broke apart; my parents moved to two different cities and sold the house when I was sixteen. I did some couch surfing and then moved in with a friend and dropped out of high school.

Though I enrolled in community college and kept going with speech and debate, I led something of a double life at that point. If you're imagining it, I probably did it. I moonlighted as a shoplifter, pot dealer, and all-around grifter. I did a little modeling that verged on the inappropriate. I was locked up for theft. I'll never forget dealing weed in a plaid schoolgirl outfit to a large black man in the shadow of a Methodist church in the South Park Blocks of Portland on a Sunday morning. Just as we were passing the money and weed across, a tiny, respectable, behatted black grandma walked by trailing clouds of descendants and lit into him for corrupting a lovely young girl. I eyed her and said, "You're so right, ma'am; he can keep those drugs," took my money, and walked away. We see what we expect to see.

I was barely hanging on in college. I spent some of my time LARPing (live-action role-playing). I met a lot of good friends playing a game called Vampire, including one very interesting man with dark eyes who had the loveliest voice. As I was a mere sixteen-year-old, he was a very unattainable and undateable twenty-seven years, but we used to stay up all night at coffee shops discussing just about anything. I was fairly good at talking about things and won gold in the national community college persuasive-speaking championship in 1997. It netted me the attention of the top speech and debate program in the country, a tiny Catholic college in Helena, Montana. I knew if I didn't leave Portland, I would die of an overdose or sink into the kind of half hostess, half hooker life I was barreling toward. I don't know how many arms the coach twisted to get me and my fairly shameful transcripts past the admissions committee, but I accepted the baller admissions offer from Carroll College, and thank heaven there was no Facebook then. I pitched my broken switchblade and a few empty bottles out the car window on the way through the mountains in Idaho toward my new state.

Montana and Carroll College saved my life. Don't get me wrong; I was viciously homesick and I whined a lot about the lack of . . . well, everything. Still, I was part of the Carroll forensics team that won the 1999 National Parliamentary Debate championship, and I got a truly outstanding liberal arts education there. At that time I started learning about the amazing technology called the "Inter-Net," which you accessed using an AOL CD and sometimes a browser window that said "Netscape Navigator" at the top. I played guitar, acted in school plays, learned Chinese kenpo karate, and taught myself to cook. At a philosophy conference, I won a theological essay contest in the morning and performed as the dancing slave girl at the fourth-century reenactment banquet that evening. I built elaborate Dungeons & Dragons campaigns for my local game shop and dungeon-mastered them. The field of international relations seduced me away from the communications degree I had started. I'd begun circling around a question I keep asking myself even now: What makes people do what they do?

I then went to Portland State University for my MS in political science. I sweated over cognitive behavioral theory, applied economics, strategies of warfare, small-arms transfers, and a hell of a lot of calculus, statistics, computational simulation, and game theory. It was here that I began a torrid love affair with the social sciences. This extraordinary education included some very important principles, like expected utility theory and cognitive bias via prospect theory, the Nobel Prize–winning combination of economics and psychology created by Amos Tversky and Daniel Kahneman in the 1980s and 1990s. If you really understand unconscious bias and underlying economic incentives, it makes you able to identify and predict some kinds of human behavior. Game theory is cool.

Turns out that some of those skills are useful in a little game called poker too.

I stormed off to do my doctorate in complex systems and political science at the University of Michigan. Think of this degree as the unholy amalgamation of applied mathematics, computer science, evolutionary biology, and game theory applied to international warfare. I was surrounded by some of the smartest people in the world and learned an unbelievable amount, but I was too miserable and out of place socially to appreciate it. Michigan is an elite school, and I was often surrounded by students who had wealth managers and real-estate investments. I had no idea how to fit in and reacted about as awkwardly and poorly as possible. I was very, very lonely, so I joined the Argentine tango club on campus. I spent a lot of nights in dark basements tangoing with strangers. I wish I could have finished my doctorate, but the institutional support, loans, and health care disappeared four years in. I have a bad back, and I started breaking apart physically and emotionally after some incidents on campus. I finally skulked back home in 2008.

I was back in Oregon, exhausted, broke, burned out, sleeping on my mom's floor, and feeling like a complete failure, now with a heavy helping of student-loan debt—but also with a set of technical skills that were much, much more marketable than I realized. I had been coding all along, and I started doing more web development. I moved to Seattle to take a job as a lead web dev for Microsoft Game Studios for an Xbox game. After that, I worked on the Halo team and elevated myself to bigger and bigger jobs.

From time to time I'd thought of the big, quiet, dark-eyed man I'd met while gaming as a teenager back in Portland, and it turned out that he'd thought of me too—and that he lived in Seattle. We friended each other on Facebook on Valentine's Day 2009, and the first message he sent to me was "How are you still single???"

Reader, I married the hell out of him.

In 2012 I was also running my web development company, Red Queen Technologies, in Seattle and taking clients to pay the bills, when one client wanted a large web application built. I hired a brilliant Seattle developer I'd met at a tango dance, Liz Dahlstrom, to help me develop some of the application. I knew that I didn't have the information security expertise needed to protect the client's data, so I proposed to my client that he send us to a large infosec conference to either get the training we needed or network with some people with an eye to hiring them. I did a bit of research within my budget constraints and found that the biggest annual infosec conference, DEF CON, was coming up quickly. I packed myself and Liz off to Las Vegas for the twentieth DEF CON. One hour after arriving, I fell down the rabbit hole.

We met infosec pros, all right. We joined a crew called the Psychoholics, spent all weekend competing in crazed mental Olympics for hackers, and won. I learned to pick locks and handcuffs (a skill which would have come in handy quite a few times earlier in life—and those are some very good stories I'm not going to recount here). I've been back every year since. I love the mental agility and total disregard for authority that my hacker family has when looking for answers and exploring the world. These people are now some of my dearest friends and most respected colleagues, and I'm profoundly grateful to have found them.

My experiences in the Seattle area as a contractor since 2009 had made me aware that there was something different and difficult about being a woman in the technical field. I had always been in academic programs that were light on women; I was usually the only woman in the room, but since my grades in academia were based on objective tests that I always aced, I never felt discriminated against. In tech, I was still the only woman in the room, but something was different. Up until I started working in tech, I had barely acknowledged the existence of sexism. Because I had not experienced it myself, I believed that it wasn't real, or that if it was, it was not as widespread, endemic, and debilitating as other people (obviously more lazy and whiny than me, I thought) were making it out to be. When my eyes were truly opened to sexism in information technology, I knew I needed to act. For the first time, people questioned my capacity to be a scientist, an engineer, a systems designer, and an architect, all because I was female.

The experiences I had interviewing for those tech contracts led to my work in mentoring women and minorities in tech, and to my discovery of a gaping market inefficiency in the business-to-business world. It turned out that no one had yet built a way to handle truly paperless employee management, because no one technical enough to solve the problem and security-oriented enough to protect the data had felt the pain of the time lost in pen-and-paper logistics and management of humans. Liz and I co-founded Fizzmint in August of 2012 after we prototyped a document-processing application together. It took a social scientist to see the hole in the market.

I've left out huge chunks of my story. The reason I started writing this book to begin with was to explore why women go into tech and why they stay there in spite of all the barriers that still exist and seem to be growing. I've told these stories about why I'm here in tech still and why I'm not leaving. Come find me some time, and I'll tell you about the biker-bar fights, the crashed cars, the rock stars, the night I crawled on a piano while singing Peggy Lee, the time I broke an entire Intel computer lab, my pet tarantula Binky, and that one trip to Istanbul when I met . . . well, you get the idea.

I can't stop asking questions, and I can't stop fighting waste and unconscious social bias. I usually drop by the end of the day. I have spent too much time afraid, alone, exhausted, and miserable, and I'm finally happy now. I don't want to save my energy. I want to burn every single day of my life down to the ground and dance howling in the ashes. I can sleep later, when I'm in stasis on the Mars colony ship.

I'm not standard; I'm deviant. But I'm not alone. I'm a complete freak of nature, and I emerged from a set of circumstances that are improbable on an astronomic scale. The same is probably true for you too. Buffy the Vampire Slayer always wanted to be just a normal girl, and maybe I did, too, just a little. Normal girls don't have an exciting life, though, and they don't break trail. If I can sum up everything I know into a single piece of wisdom, it's these words from the mother of modern computing, USN Rear Admiral Grace M. Hopper, PhD: "It is better to beg forgiveness than ask permission."

DOT MATRIX

<APPLYING FOR JOBS and the TECH RÉSUMÉ>

Welcome to technology! If you are just now getting out of your college or training program or have taught yourself a programming language, you're probably thinking that it's time to get a job. Here's the thing: tech job listings on any website are bewildering. They rarely have any information in them about the job you'd actually be doing and often have weird language in them intended to filter for the "right" people. I'll show you how to understand these job descriptions so you can apply for the ones that will be good fits. Then, we will go over the ideal tech résumé so you have your first weapon in hand in your quest to get hired.

WHICH COMPANIES SHOULD I WORK FOR?

A company you actually want to work for includes three things in its job description: the duties you'd have, the minimum qualifications, and the preferred qualifications. These are usually bullet points, and they're listed in order of priority. If each of these areas has five items and you have the first item of each of the three areas covered, you should apply for the job. You should treat the remaining four items as suggestions or nice-to-haves. Most of the time, the person writing the job description has nothing to do with hiring the developer, and the hiring manager won't even look at the job description. The minimum qualifications section isn't even really "minimum" qualifications. Everything past that first bullet under minimum is a nice-to-have, and you can demonstrate the rest as needed. I'm going to tell you about bad job descriptions first so you can spot them easily, and then the good versions.

Bad Job Descriptions

Often you will see nonsense in job descriptions such as "Ruby ninja" or "Java rockstar." If you see "ninja" or "rockstar" in the job description, toss it. They are code words that mean "We don't pay enough, but the environment is so cool and our product so hot that you should be grateful to work here and put in hundred-hour work-weeks." These words are commonly found in job postings for video game developers and stealth-mode startups being run by overgrown teenagers to whom someone's given a blank check. Run a long way in the opposite direction.

Other nonsense words or phrases like "self-starter" and "leader in the absence of leadership" are commonly found in job descriptions and can be interpreted as "our environment is chaotic, and you must have a sixth sense for which of the many tasks you will be assigned will actually matter, and which you will be criticized for completing when other higher-priority tasks needed doing." These words are copied and pasted from other job descriptions, and they sound good to HR. Here's an example of a terrible job listing. As you can see, there's no list of nice-to-haves, which means that whatever thoughtless human put this on the web actually thinks that a person who fits all these qualifications could possibly exist.

We're looking for an ambitious and adaptable Python developer experienced in the ins and outs of development in a team setting. As part of our Engineering Development group based in Austin, TX, you will be working individually and collaboratively to develop, implement, and support custom solutions through fast-paced, dynamic projects involving components at every level of the [redacted] platform to extend its functionality to meet our clients' unique needs. Our ideal candidate is someone with a self-motivated tinkering spirit and who is comfortable diving into professional development life while rapidly learning to engineer solutions using a mix of open technologies and our own proprietary framework.

RESTRICTIONS
- No telecommuting
- Agencies are OK

REQUIREMENTS
- 3–5 years of software development experience
- Proficiency in Python and SQL
- Web development experience
- Passion for applying good design principals while exercising pragmatism to keep deadlines
- Experience in all aspects of the software development life cycle
- Experience engineering software in a service-oriented architecture
- Strong analytical and problem-solving skills
- Effective communication skills
- Experience contributing in an Agile development environment
- Good interpersonal skills
- Occasional availability for on-call/emergency support
- Ability to work flexible hours when necessary for deadlines and off-hours installations

The first thing to know is that what they actually want is a Python developer who has some experience slurping data from any SQL database application. The rest of it is all nice-to-haves. The fact that *they* don't realize it is the real problem. No human being can possibly have all these traits, and there are several very clear warning signs here:

1. "Individually and collaboratively" means that they don't have a solid management structure that can mentor and help you.
2. Anyone who straight-facedly uses the words "fast-paced, dynamic" in a job description copied and pasted boilerplate and never even talked to the actual dev team. (I'm getting an inspiration at this point to create Horrible Job Listing Bingo.)
3. "Passion for applying good design principals [sic] while exercising pragmatism to keep deadlines" means that you're going to be faced with impossible choices between coding the right way and meeting the unrealistic expectations of your manager.
4. If they actually have to say that you'll work odd hours to meet deadlines and for client-related emergencies, run. Just run.

Good Job Descriptions

So, what does it look like when someone has put thought into a job listing? My friend Dan Shapiro has a desktop laser-cutter company called Glowforge. They make very, very cool tech, and I just saw Glowforge post a job description for the web developer they'd like to hire. This is the right way to do it:

WHAT YOU'LL BE DOING:
- Writing bucketloads of high quality code (naturally).
- We already use Rails & Python but have a lot more work to do. You'll help drive the decisions about what technologies to add to the stack.

- You'll work closely with the hardware team to understand the capabilities of our product and help unlock its potential.
- You'll participate in planning sessions with the whole product team and can help build the user stories, requirements and specifications that will drive development.
- You'll be building the software to fabricate the future[—]not just another CRUD app.

YOUR QUALIFICATIONS:
- You've been responsible for shipping a product that people love.
- You're thoughtful about systems engineering, design patterns, and algorithms.
- You're passionate about writing great software . . . and still know that you sometimes have to make some tradeoffs to ship quickly.

NICE TO HAVES:
- Back-end server technologies and designing for the *ilities (testability, maintainability, extensibility, scalability, and security-ility).
- Hardware experience like drivers, motion controller algorithms, and/or low-level code (you'll be working closely with the hardware team and may have the opportunity to build low-level interfaces).
- Graphics experience (for some cool, secret stuff that we can't talk about in a public job posting).
- Javascript, CSS, and HTML (big chunks of our product are user-facing web software).

Here's what tells you that someone put thought into this (Dan Shapiro wishes to credit Textio, an app developed by Kieran Snyder, with helping him remove biased language and create a good listing):

1. The only thing that you know will absolutely be required is the very first item, which is that you have been responsible for shipping a product that people love. If you've done that, the

Glowforge people know that you have a whole list of associated traits like responsibility, technical ability, and an eye for design and picking good projects.

2. The nice-to-haves are the things that often appear as requirements in other listings, but here show up as optional. The reason for this is that this team is looking for a person with a particular set of personal and professional traits and is fine with them learning tech on the job. Once you've learned programming and how to ship a product, basically all technologies are dialects that you can pick up as you go.

When you see a job listing ask for soft skills like "community minded," "helpful," "cheerful," and other words that describe a team player without actually using the wildly annoying phrase "team player," you may have found a company that does care about culture and the experience you'll have working there. Why do companies ask for soft skills? After all, as a developer, you are there to write code, right? Not so much. In any corporate environment, you must be an advocate for yourself and for your team. It is more important for a developer to be likable than to be a genius. Geniuses do not make good colleagues. If a developer is not likable and easy to work with, meaning calm, nonconfrontational, and receptive to positive and negative feedback, they will find themselves edged out of team-building outings like lunches and after-dinner drinks. That leads to a lack of promotion and eventually to obsolescence and being shown the door. This company is trying to build a good culture and a good place to work, and they're filtering for people who care about kindness and professionalism, rather than for developers who will write acres of amazing code while poisoning the air for everyone else around them. There are very, very few exceptions to this rule, and they usually involve famous programmers and inventors who are often totally removed from a team and put in what the industry sometimes calls "titanium silos of excellence."

They're rare beasts, and I don't recommend trying to emulate them as a career strategy.

Part of why I'm giving you a simple heuristic for the jobs to which you should apply is that the process of applying for your first job is like throwing darts at an invisible board. You may or may not hit, or someone may notice something about you that makes you a great fit for a job that hasn't been posted yet. As long as you apply en masse, it's a numbers game, and you may get interviews or at least phone screens, which will start to build your comfort with the process of interviewing. The world is headed away from long-term, full-time salaried employment, and your chances of interviewing for jobs on a yearly or very regular basis are going up, so it pays to get comfortable with this process.

THE TECH RÉSUMÉ

Now you've found twenty or so job postings that you'd be interested in exploring further. Every one of them will require a résumé from you, but let's be honest: no one actually reads those résumés anymore. At first, your résumé will only be put into a database and parsed for keywords. The only time someone will actually skim through your résumé is when you are sitting across from each other in an interview (or possibly during a phone interview). There is no reason to be afraid or obsessive about your résumé, because ultimately you and your code are your résumé, and the actual piece of paper matters very little. Still, it's a hurdle you'll have to leap in order to get your first job. Here's how to make this process as easy as possible.

A tech résumé is different from all other résumés in its format, usage, and purpose. You will create a bulleted list that is an overview of your skills and major accomplishments first (but never your previous pay rates), submitting both a text and a PDF (portable document format) version of your résumé. The first thing to remember is that almost none of the eyes that see your résumé will be human. Your résumé will be machine-processed many dozens if not hundreds of times more than a person will read it, and every single word counts. One comment: don't bother with cover letters. It takes too much time to write one for each company, and I've never heard of a technologist being hired or not based on a cover letter. While it may have happened, it's unlikely to be worth your effort.

How to Optimize Your Résumé for Mass Applications to Jobs

You need to make your résumé as long as possible with lots of details under each job. The days of the one-page résumé are gone; in tech, you should include all your relevant skills, every major activity and project you've ever done, and any additional information about how you apply your skills, because humans aren't the ones reading it. Senior contractors and developers often have six- to eight-page résumés, including all their professional certifications and each major project completed at every job. My résumé (which I update on a monthly basis even though I'm the CEO of a startup) is somewhere around seven pages long. If yours is too short, it will not provide the detail needed to a hiring manager, and worse, when résumé databases are machine-parsed for specific skill sets, your résumé will not be pulled up.

It's common to be asked to provide star levels for skills. Your years of experience aren't as relevant as your level of expertise, and it's usually done on a five-star basis. If you are a core contributor to the Python language, you're a five star. If you have taken three or four online tutorials in Python, you're a one star. If you have done some work professionally or have taken a class on Python, you are a two star or possibly a three. You can use your own judgment, but do be aware that you may be harder on yourself than a hiring manager will be. Ask someone else to help you assign your star levels to your skills. You will often be surprised and pleased at another person's opinion of your abilities.

Put a text version of your résumé online. Contractors get work through people searching for them, and if you are excellent in your field, you will pop to the top of search results for "$CITY $SKILL $JOB_TITLE." Contractors now get a significant portion of their jobs from people actually searching for them personally, and unless you have a reason not to post your text-based résumé online, such as a fear of retribution from your current employer, do so and keep it updated at all times. One intuitive way to do it is to put your résumé up at yoursite.com/resume. I was once one of the top Google results for "Seattle web developer," and I got great job offers as a result.

When you describe how you "delivered specs for multilayer architecture before the deadline," try to include the number of days before the deadline by which you delivered the project. It gives your skills and accomplishments real punch to show actual numbers. People believe numbers in a way that they do not believe declarative statements, and this is a good area to use some careful psychological adjustment on the person reading your résumé. There are places on my résumé where I've included general achievements but have forgotten the dates or times, and I wish I had been editing my résumé once a month for longer so that I could add these kinds of numbers.

Have a community service section of some kind. Companies are focusing more and more on the full lives of their workforce. If you do not volunteer in some way, ensure that you include your participation in community groups such as open source projects, help forums for the technologies in which you have skills, and your mentorship of others. If you do not mentor younger developers, start doing so (see the Mentorship chapter), and list it on your résumé. In addition, your participation in open source projects and online mentorship of younger technologists in your field can be easily checked, and like your online repository and portfolio, shows that you know your field very well.

Curate and polish your initial skills section until it positively gleams. Almost nothing in your résumé besides that first skills section and your previous job titles will be read by an actual human. Those first ten bullet points that go right at the top under your name and contact information and that include your job title and your major accomplishments and skills are the part of the résumé that humans will be reading and to which they will actually pay attention. You should have no typos anywhere on your résumé, and you should manicure this section in particular to obsessive levels to make yourself sound confident and appealing. Go to my website to see my résumé, which is an example of a skills-based résumé. This is a very, very good format for technologists, because it hides a multitude of sins, like odd gaps in my timeline and strange job-title progression.

Put your skills overview and your work history first, since a hiring manager will be looking at these two sections the most. If your education or detailed skills come first, the interviewer might miss your skills overview since they expect history first. Order your skills section with your best skills on top. Interviewers will assume your best skills are listed first. While this is not a problem with machines, a human will arrange or approve your interview based on your top-listed skills.

Bullet everything. If you don't, your interviewer will have a giant wall of text to read. Your bullet points, especially in the overview section, should be no more than a couple of lines each. You're breaking up the text so that there are no paragraphs—which people skim without really reading. The first few words of each bullet point are the most important; they should include numbers and action verbs. This means your résumé will read as a history of your achievements. Begin your bullets with action verbs like developed, coded, programmed, installed, uploaded, altered, controlled, designed, architected, delivered, provided, ordered, analyzed, and achieved (use that one sparingly) that will help people see you as competent and able to clearly state what you've done in your career.

Major Don'ts

Don't include irrelevant jobs or skills. Examples of these would be work-study positions, high school fast-food jobs, collegiate competitive sports or high school service awards, and nontechnical extracurricular activities. Even if your résumé has only a few items, they should be relevant to your tech field. Your programming- and tech-class projects do count as skills and achievements, and you should absolutely list them in thorough detail, especially if you are proud of them and they're in your portfolio. For people who have been out of tech for some time, do not include jobs that might seem nontechnical. If you wanted to keep working as an advertising executive, you would have. If you want to get into tech, work experience that's unrelated to technology is likely to make your hiring manager think you have a short attention span. If you have name-brand tech companies on your résumé and can present your work as having been technical, that's a little different. In that case, you might have a great network at your previous companies, which is an asset to your future companies. The best advice is to include only technical work and skills, and to exclude any work that is not technical.

Do not send your résumé in Word format to any company other than Microsoft unless you've been specifically instructed to do so. If you're applying to Apple, you could send your résumé as a Pages document. Other than that, send a PDF and a text file. Your file format can be seen as a declaration of allegiance (yes, really), and in the Microsoft community, sending a .doc or .docx is expected.

Outside that community, many developers may not look favorably on a Word file, since the proportion of technical people who use Word and MS Office is far, far lower than the general population. The Word version of your résumé may be unreadable or garbled in a text reader. That same reader will parse and chew up your résumé based on very elaborate Boolean queries from recruiters and hiring managers, so don't worry too much about the look of the text file. It should look decent in text format, but everyone understands that the PDF is intended to be the pretty version of your résumé. Use asterisks for bullet points in the text file. Your résumé should look basically the same in text as it does in a PDF, and using creative fonts will only irritate your hiring manager or any person who looks at your résumé. Only graphic designers need to worry about how their résumé looks, and if I'm hiring graphic or web designers, the thing I'm most interested in is whether they understand how to use white space on their résumé. That tells me all I need to know about whether they're careful and have good design sense.

Avoid using self-limiting words like "entry level," "junior," or "starting." There is no such thing as a "Starting Web Developer" when it comes to job titles, and if someone sees these words on your résumé, they will assume you are more junior than you may be. Even if you are applying to your very first job, you have some experience as a software developer, or you would not be applying. Tech is not like airplane maintenance, where not having had the job title before means that you have never done it. Instead, think of yourself as average until proven otherwise, and ensure that your skill levels are clearly marked on your résumé in each of your skill areas (using stars as we discussed earlier, not years of experience).

Do not include your previous pay levels or salaries. They will limit you when it comes to negotiations. You are worth whatever you can get a company to pay you. The best way to price yourself is to keep raising your required salary or per-hour wage until you stop being able to come to an agreement with companies making you offers. We will talk more about this in the Types of Tech Jobs and Salary Negotiations chapter.

If you are required to enter in your previous salaries in a job application form such as Taleo, a database that is heavily used by recruiters, put in zeros. If a person at a company demands your previous salary level, do not apply there. That is a company more interested in getting you cheap than treating you well with a market-appropriate salary. There are very few reasons to flatly refuse to interview or interact with a company, and this is one of them.

A giant mistake frequently made by younger people or much older returning tech workers is unprofessional contact information or an inappropriate email address. A good fallback email address is Gmail, but the truth is that any software developer who doesn't use name@fullname.com or name@mybigawesomeproject.com as an email address is starting with a black mark. If you have only a school email address, do not include it on your résumé; get a personal site and use that email address. Setting up Google Apps with a domain name is dead easy and takes less than five minutes—too easy, in fact, for you to still be using iheartcatvideos@aol.com or j.doe@statetechuniversity.edu. There are people who say they don't care what email address a person has, and if they're telling the truth, having a good email doesn't help or hurt you—but having a poor one will hurt you if someone does in fact care.

Get rid of your objective. No objective other than "I want to be the next president of the United States" has ever sounded snappy and attractive anyway. It is also busywork, and you have to change it each time you submit it. Use your desired title instead: "Senior Web Developer and Systems Architect" sounds better than any objective. It doesn't have to be a title you've held before at a job; it can be the title you give yourself based on your current skill set.

Typos. Your résumé will be round-filed without question or appeal. If you cannot be sure that your résumé, which is an introduction letter to your prospective team, is free of simple errors, companies won't want you touching code—and nor do I.

There are tiny misspellings that can cost you an interview—e.g., "C Sharp Dot Net" instead of "C#.NET." This happens because database parsers are looking for very specific combinations of skill sets and acronyms. Your résumé will never be read if you fail to use common spellings or if you have transposed a letter—e.g., "HMTL." A human eye would read "HMTL" with no problem whatsoever. Many studies have been done on how people read only the first and last letter of many common words, and in context, most people would not even notice that typo. A computer, however, will never display your résumé if a hiring manager is looking for web developers.

Do not include months when you add dates for your jobs. Contract work in technology is increasing, and it is common to take a break of some kind between contracts. It's not unusual for technologists to work at multiple companies over the course of a year and to work for only part of the year, especially as their skill sets improve and they do more consulting and higher-skilled work. Nevertheless, gaps in employment can still be misunderstood by someone who does not understand the tech career track—and that can certainly include an HR person who actually works at a tech company. If you have breaks in your work history of more than a year, consider including a freelance or volunteer tech project as part of your work history or forming your own company.

Don't include any personal information besides your email address, phone number, and possibly your mailing address (but not your home address). Your résumé is not the place to list your marital status, number of children, sexual orientation, political affiliation, or religion. If any of the job titles or volunteer positions you have included in your résumé imply personal information about you (e.g., PTA volunteer, NRA activist, Lutheran church choir, Greenpeace), think hard about how to rephrase them as neutral titles. If you developed a website as a PTA volunteer, consider phrasing your position as "education service organization technical volunteer" or in some other way to depersonalize your affiliations. No matter how proud a parent you are, talking about your children will almost certainly hurt you and will never help you as a woman, though the opposite is often true for men. Interviewers will never admit that they passed on you because you have four children, and most of the time, they won't even realize they discriminated against you.

Do not make demands regarding salary or benefits on your résumé. It's a bad idea for the same reason that including personal information is. You could be limiting yourself as well as being excluded from jobs for which you might have been a good fit and been able to negotiate good benefits.

Avoid overcapitalization (meaning capitalizing many or all words in achievements or skills that are not proper nouns, titles, acronyms, or the beginnings of bullet points). Personally, I think it is harsh on the eye and signals an overcompensating personality type. I don't have any data to back up my opinion on this other than anecdotes, but the résumé reviewers I've talked to have all agreed with me on this.

Do not use the word "potential" anywhere on your résumé; that is grounds for having it immediately discarded.

Don't use big words and superlatives to cover a lack of real skill. Here's an example: "Provided my broad and deep multiyear technical expertise to solve difficult design problems." That statement is worthless to a technologist. Here is the useful version: "Used Android SDK to mock up a mobile application to resolve cross-platform interface design conflict." If you have ever taken a writing course of any kind, you have likely heard the maxim "show, don't tell." That is an excellent philosophy for writing your résumé. Show your skill, the problem you solved, and how it benefited the project.

Don't use a conversational style; it's not a good idea in tech. In many career paths, using personal pronouns or full sentences (such as "I enjoyed my time at X Inc. While there, I felt my potential was being used to its fullest effect") may be appropriate, but on a tech résumé, there should be no personal pronouns and hardly any full sentences.

There's no need to include a keywords section. If you have not listed HTML as one of your skills, including it as a keyword would look strange. All keywords you would use should be included in your skills section and the bullet points under each of your jobs anyway.

Don't include the names and contact information of your references on a résumé that you're going to blast out into dozens of databases. You'll be the cause of people you really need to like you getting spammed. Instead, simply write "References available upon request" at the end of your résumé; that is the de facto closing statement for a long résumé anyway. (People have strong feelings about this. Some people hate it, and others don't mind it. The only real error would be to include contact info for your references. You can choose to leave off this statement if you want; I have left it on mine but might take it off eventually if the fashion swings all the way over to a total absence of references to references—pun intended.) In addition, you will want to select the people who can recommend you for each individual job based on their network and connections to the company. There are a few exceptions to this rule. If you're coming out of an internship with a prestigious company and a well-known technologist has agreed to recommend you, you can use that name to give your résumé a little extra hype. At the point when prospective employers are checking references, they'll do an Internet search on you and see who you know and interact with online anyway.

Do not include graphics of any kind on your résumé. No borders, no smiley faces, no hearts, no pictures of any kind (including your headshot). While saying that your résumé should be formatted as a text file should make this point quite obvious, remember that any graphics on your résumé may misalign your text, remove any credibility your experience and skills may give you as an IT professional, and absolutely shred the composure of any hiring manager who is reading your résumé. Use only caps for your résumé title; bold for your name, job titles, and educational institutions; italics for dates; asterisks for bullet points; and any special symbols needed for your programming languages.

Including a summary paragraph at the end of your résumé means that you think your skills and previous experience are insufficient or the people reading your résumé need help to understand who you are. As I said before, no paragraphs should ever appear in your résumé—only lists. If you think you need a paragraph to make your point, go back over your résumé and add in any missing skills or accomplishments under the bullet points where they belong. Your personality and interview skills, not an unread brick of text, are your summary paragraph.

Finally, never, ever, ever lie on your résumé. Rephrasing your work to show off your strong skills or to remove unnecessary personal information is very different than flat-out lying about what you have done and where you have done it. Any falsehood on your résumé can be easily checked, and you will be outed as a liar. That is a reputation that, in the age of social media, can follow you all your life. You can live down a drunken toga party pic (ask me how!). However, you will not escape a reputation for dishonesty on your résumé. In addition, unlike for many jobs, you must have some very specific and immediately testable skills to work in tech, and whether or not you can code is just as ridiculously easy to check as whether you ever had a .edu email address from the school you say you attended. While you must portray confidence in your skills to successfully interview for tech jobs—often more confidence than you may actually feel at the time—do not ever claim to have a degree or certification that you do not or to have worked in a job position that you have not. It is deeply wrong and unethical, and people will never give you a second chance if you lie about graduating from Harvard or being a software engineer at Google. You'd create legal liability for any company that hired you if they knew you'd lied on your résumé, and no one would take that chance on you ever again.

Actually, You Won't Need a Résumé at All

Your résumé is not your résumé. In reality, your code is your résumé. If your code is up at an online repository such as GitHub, absolutely include that address in your résumé up at the very top. The résumé is required paperwork for a job, but you will be hired (or not) based on what you have done, not based on your document-formatting skills. You'll be discovered and recruited based on the people you know and the conferences you've attended, not through applying to jobs on websites. We'll talk more in the Networking and Relationships and Personal Branding chapters about how you'll really get jobs after your very first one.

If you've followed these rules, and you've formatted your résumé like mine or any other skills-based résumé, you've given yourself the best possible chance to make it through to tech interviews at companies you'd love to work for. Check my personal website for my résumé or an example résumé.

THE DEVELOPER
Kamilah Taylor

"Wi likkle but wi tallawah." A common expression in my home country of Jamaica, the general sentiment is "We may be small, but don't discount us, because we're strong." Jamaicans believe that we can truly do anything on a global scale, which is how we've invented music genres, broken world records, and won international singing competitions and spelling bees. This was instilled in me at a young age.

As a child, I climbed trees, read books, played with Legos, created imaginary kingdoms with my Barbies, did art, solved puzzles, and played computer games on our prized Macintosh—Kid Pix, Word Munchers, and Number Munchers were my favorites. I started piano, which I still play, at the age of five, and I was in the choir, so I'd go around the house singing. I also loved math and got the idea in my head that I wanted to go to space—maybe because *Star Trek: The Next Generation* was on TV those days. One day I declared that I wanted to be either an astronaut or a singer, and my mom told me that I had to do science if I wanted to be an astronaut. I remember thinking to myself: I think I'll choose the life of math and science. I actually first coded somewhere between the ages of seven and nine in the Logo programming language.

When we moved to Atlanta, I went through culture shock. Back home, I didn't have to fight to get into more advanced math and science classes, and nobody cared that I was a girl—gender just isn't as much of a sticking point in Jamaica, which has the highest percentage of female managers in the world. It was a whole new game. Despite my doing well in sixth-grade math, my teacher simply neglected to tell me or my parents that I could skip ahead to pre-algebra in seventh grade. When we asked her why, she told us she thought we wouldn't be interested.

It got a little better when I attended North Springs High School, a performing arts and sciences magnet school that is now a charter school. Even then, I faced a few unsupportive math and science teachers who insisted that I would only ever be a B student and only gave leadership opportunities to other students. I was lucky to get two wonderful teachers starting in my junior year, though: Timothy Maley, my Intro to Computer Science and Advanced Placement Physics teacher, and Joan Newell, my Advanced Placement Calculus teacher. Mr. Maley taught me robotics, something I'd already started playing with a year earlier when my parents gave me my first Lego Mindstorms robotics kit—but more than that, he recognized something in me. I'll never forget the moment he singled me out and asked me first, before anyone else in the class, if I'd be interested in participating in a robotics competition being held at Georgia Tech. When I coasted through with a high B in my AP Calculus class, Ms. Newell wrote on my report card that I could do better—and I did.

By the time I got to AP Computer Science in my senior year, I was already pretty sure I wanted to study math and computer science in college. I never had any concerns about my ability to do computer science. In fact, I found it kind of easy. The one concern I had was my impression of people who studied computer science. The techie guys were pretty unkind to us girls, and I actually saw one of them tell a girl that she only got into Yale because of affirmative action. I was also tired of feeling like an immigrant and out of place, so I decided to go ahead with CS and math but back home in Jamaica.

I have no regrets about this decision. I would never have had the connection I have to Jamaica if I hadn't attended university there, or the perspective on the different attitudes to race and gender in the sciences in my years outside the United States. I was one of the top students in math, physics, and computer science, and me being female was never an issue. During my freshman year, I bought Brian Greene's *The Elegant Universe* and fell in love with string theory. That summer I couldn't pick between my three loves, and I was two classes short of a minor in physics, but in the end I graduated with a double major in math and computer science.

I was convinced that my career path was to attend university and graduate school, get a PhD, and be a professor. The only question was what exactly to study in graduate school. I'd been struggling trying to do it all, but this was the moment to choose. After years of robotics as a hobby, I decided to pursue it full time and do a PhD in computer science specializing in robotics. I got into three of my top five choices and ended up choosing the University of Illinois at Urbana-Champaign.

Robotics was a great fit for me. I was able to combine my love of math, physics, and computer science. I worked on solving navigation and path-planning problems with simpler, cheaper, and fewer sensors than were traditionally assumed to be necessary. Academia, however, was less of a good fit. I loved being able to define my own problems and come up with solutions, but looking back, I think the lack of structure was difficult for me.

I had another challenge—the pressure of being the minority in the department. There was only one other black woman in the computer science PhD program, and I was the only Jamaican, so it felt like I was representing three groups of people. When things were going well, this was great. When things got hard, this became a stumbling block. I'd keep thinking that if I failed or did not do as well on anything, it would reflect poorly on black people, on women, and on Jamaicans. This was, of course, ridiculous, but when I was in the middle of the program, it felt like reality, and I struggled.

One day, I realized that I'd never been this unhappy and that I couldn't evaluate my life based on the degrees I had. I took a step back, deleted the notion that I had to have a PhD, finished the requirements for the master's degree, and made the decision to take a year off.

Searching for that first job was hard. As an international student, I had a ticking timer, and my specialization led to many jobs that had government funding. Still, I got two offers and made yet another career decision—to pick the job as a software engineer for a robotics project at a software company, as opposed to the job at a robotics company. I saw that putting myself in such a narrow field that was still very young would make it difficult to find jobs, and what I really wanted was to be challenged with interesting problems—they didn't have to deal with robotics. So I started my first job at Wolfram Research, makers of Mathematica and Wolfram|Alpha. On that first day, I found a Lego Mindstorms kit on my desk, and I knew that this was the right decision.

At Wolfram, I had a little more structure and still got to define a lot of my early work, but I sensed very early that it was somewhere I could get comfortable and stay forever, and I knew I wanted something different. I was finally starting to figure out what I did and didn't want in my career. I stayed on while my robotics project was still going, but once that got canceled (what it became can be seen in the Wolfram Connected Devices Project), it was time to move west and go all in on my career as a software engineer.

As an undergrad, I was the vice president and then president of the electronics club. During my tenure as president, I really wanted to enter a robotics maze competition, but I think I was the person most enthusiastic about it. My friends were interested but not as into it, and I ended up frustrated that I wasn't able to make the club spend the summer and time outside of classes working on our robot. In the end, it very nearly cost me some friendships that I managed to repair eventually, and I shied away from being a vocal leader after this. This came back to haunt me when I landed at LinkedIn. I'd gotten into a habit of trying not to stand out too much due to feeling like a triple minority and my earlier failed experience at leading. In Silicon Valley, especially as a woman, if you don't assert yourself, you'll never get the great projects, or get to lead, or get the promotions. It took a manager saying "You should really lead this little project" for it to get in my head that I knew enough to take on larger roles.

It didn't help that for the longest time, I felt like a beginner. When I started, I felt as if everyone else knew so much more than I did about making a website that is as large and as complex as LinkedIn. My manager encouraged me to ask questions, but in my head I thought that if I asked too many questions, everyone would wonder how I got this job, and they'd discover that I didn't know as much as they did. It was classic impostor syndrome. My first project was mobile registration—the first time I'd worked in mobile web. Just as I'd gotten comfortable executing in that space, the project was over, and I moved on to Profile 2.0, the revamp of the LinkedIn profile page in 2012, written in Java and Dust.js. Once more, just as I'd gotten comfortable with that stack, that project was over, and this time I was given the choice between a couple of projects. I picked the first iteration of the LinkedIn Connected app for iOS, one of the first native apps at LinkedIn and the first in our family of apps that was not the flagship app. I bought a bunch of iOS and Objective-C books and taught myself iOS at night and on weekends while working on the project. This time, I was the one that placed myself at the beginner level, but it was a risk that has paid dividends. By the time LinkedIn started the company-wide mobilization initiative in 2014, I had mobile experience and was able to train other engineers on iOS development and mentor them as they did mobile projects on their own teams.

The years have been full of rich experiences, highs and lows, and I've emerged at the three-year mark at LinkedIn as a different person—someone seen as a leader, who actively seeks out ways to lead projects, collaborates well on a team, and has technical depth.

In the end, I can say that I am where I am because I'm pretty stubborn. I always know that I can do more and be more, and I'm too stubborn to give that up. I've found a job where I can be creative that's relaxed enough for me to have a lot of fun doing the job but fast paced enough for there to be a real energy and momentum.

Being at LinkedIn has also given me a platform to give back to the community. Because of my experience, I feel strongly about encouraging, teaching, and mentoring young people from under-represented communities—especially at the middle school and high school level. I've worked with Black Girls Code, Technovation, Code2040, and Boys and Girls Clubs of the Peninsula—all wonderful organizations that are reaching talented young people early on. I often wish I could do more, but I know that whatever I can give back counts. In the Technovation Challenge, I taught a team of high school girls how to code and mentored them for sixteen weeks through the process of building an app, making a business plan, and pitching the app. Recently I found out that two of the girls on that team got into university and have chosen to study computer science—a huge win!

The energy I feel at LinkedIn is an energy I feel throughout Silicon Valley. I noticed it in my first week and fell in love with it. There is no other place that has such a critical mass of people who are all trying to create the next big thing, invent the latest technology, and improve and scale the products and tools people use around the world. I love being a part of it, and I'm inspired to be an even bigger part of it. I'm constantly working on side projects, exploring ideas, brainstorming with others, and talking with start-ups. What's next? Who knows. Still, I know it will be great.

Three years after dropping out of my PhD program, I had a moment of inspiration on a plane. I was looking over some of the sentences I'd jotted down in my notebook, and I saw one that sparked an idea. For the rest of the flight I typed furiously, gathering my thoughts, and a product emerged. I don't know if I'll ever turn it into a reality or if someone else will get there first or if it's even feasible, but I do love that feeling. It was a feeling I had when I came up with the core algorithm in my first research paper, which ended up becoming my master's thesis. On the plane, I had an intense moment of relief as I realized that this feeling is what I loved and that I could have that outside of academia. I've had so many twists and turns in my career that made me feel like a failure or as if I were taking the easy way out or somehow not living up to my full potential, but now I get it. This is my career, and I shouldn't try to predict it, but I should always try to keep improving, keep learning, and have lots of fun doing it.

One of my ultimate goals in life is to use my passion for science and technology to help correct the imbalance I see in the world. I remember my fifteen-year-old self thinking that computer science was a field full of antisocial guys and my nineteen-year-old self thinking that a career in software engineering was dull and boring. I see and live the gender and race disparity in tech every day. I go back to Jamaica and see really smart kids and young adults with few opportunities and resources. Many of them are so sharp but just don't have access to college fairs or role models to show them that someone like them did this and they can too. There's one thing I'd love readers to take away from my story: I was just a kid growing up in Jamaica with dreams, and I want people to know that it's possible to dream bigger and accomplish those dreams.

FIRST LADY'S FIRST BOOK

mpnotnmokpdhoyrdkymuoconnpftctnigokbmnnmdc

<TECH INTERVIEWS>

Once upon a time, I was interviewing for a lead web developer position for a very violent and graphic video game. I was the handpicked successor of the person leaving the job, had more knowledge of the internal systems and codebase than anyone other than the person leaving, and had a great record as a contractor with the company. I danced through the technical interview. It was totally clear that I was the best person for the job. However, when the guys interviewing me asked if I'd ever played the game, I said, voice dripping with contempt, "Ew. No!"

I didn't get the job.

I'm going to talk about how you will look and act during your technical interviews in this chapter, and I'm going to make some generalizations. I am not an apologist for sexism. It exists, I've felt its painful effects, and I have been held back in my career and financial future when I was told that I didn't get the job because they couldn't envision me "being able to lead this rough team of guys" or because I'm "a little too forthright to get along well with others and have ruffled some feathers during this process." I cannot make companies change their policies, and I cannot fix a lifetime of biases in the head of your technical interviewer. I can, however, give you practical advice on how to smooth your way past some of the stumbles I've made, and give you more options for how to get into a great career in tech. I'm not telling you what I think is right or wrong, just what I've seen succeed most often. If a month from now you're getting paid three times what you were being paid before and you love your job, then everybody wins!

WOMEN EXPERIENCE TECH INTERVIEWS DIFFERENTLY

Tech interviews are the craziest experience you may ever have in tech. You'll spend ten hours in a small room demonstrating skills and algorithms that have absolutely nothing to do with any real programming task you'll ever do. You'll solve brainteasers and linked lists, and you'll talk about Mount Fuji and food supply on the International Space Station.

Unfortunately, women simply do not, as a statistical fact, come out of tech interviews with as many job offers as men do. Men conducting tech interviews may unconsciously expect a kind of swagger from other men that is unfortunately sometimes hugely penalized if displayed by women. To succeed at a tech interview, I display what men often call confidence and women often call arrogance. If women display it, it's called being bitchy or difficult or abrasive— often by all genders. You have to be confident enough to say "I'm a badass developer, and I don't know anyone else in this town who can do this particular task as well as I can." That comes over great if you're male but has sometimes ended interviews when I've done it. It's also what's gotten me my best and highest-paying jobs.

The discrimination you'll face is almost never conscious or intentional. We all have some kind of ism in us. Here's a direct quote from a hiring manager I once coached: "All she did was ask questions, even after I told her that her correct code was wrong to see if she'd stand up for herself. She just wanted to know why I thought that instead of telling me that I was wrong." I am guessing you can see here that the candidate was defusing conflict while still working through the problem with the interviewer, but that doesn't matter. She still didn't get the job. Many hiring managers equate confrontational behavior with strength and cooperative behavior with weakness. This doesn't mean that interviewers are bad people; they're just used to certain behaviors from successful programmers. They're pattern-matching to what they've seen be successful before. One effective tactic is to call them out on it by asking them to demonstrate. It shows you're willing to learn and removes any need for you to tell them they're wrong. The second effective tactic is to ask them to follow up with you later if there's not enough time to have them demonstrate right there.

I made two giant mistakes in that interview I described at the beginning of this chapter. First, I hadn't done my research on the product itself. I should never have walked into an interview with a team without having tried their product. Second, I made fun of what they all did for a living. Part of being a good teammate is not disparaging the project and insulting your future colleagues.

In the case of that violent video game, I was likely asked the question to begin with because I was female. They probably would have assumed I had played and was a fan if I was male. Women interviewing for technical positions at companies are often drilled much further on their knowledge about typically male-oriented products—whether or not they'll be supporting those products. I've heard that women were asked to draw a carburetor when applying for a web dev position at an auto dealer or to recite baseball statistics for a sports app mobile dev position. Continue to remind yourself that 99 percent of what you're facing is not conscious and take joy in your skills. It's sometimes cold comfort, but it's better than none. It's also what's gotten me wonderful jobs with spectacular and supportive coworkers.

In truth, the first three to five seconds after you've met your interviewer determine whether they'll be willing to offer you the job or not based on unconscious opinions they form about your dress, self-presentation, and nonverbal communication. After those five seconds, all you're trying to do is *not* give them a reason *not* to hire you. So let's talk about those things that affect an interviewer's unconscious biases.

HOW TO DRESS AND PRESENT YOURSELF

In an ideal world, people wouldn't have to present themselves differently than they are to get jobs. Still, we all live in this world, and we all have bills to pay. I've been in really bad situations, and given a choice between being hungry and wearing clothes I don't like, I know exactly which choice I have repeatedly made. So here are the lessons I've learned that you can choose to apply (or not) in your own life and career.

Don't wear suits. There is no tech company where it is appropriate to wear any kind of suit for a technical interview. (IBM might still require its interviewees to wear suits, but I haven't heard whether that policy has changed. IBM also arguably isn't really a tech-focused company.) You cannot code comfortably in a suit, which means that your interviewer will think you are putting on a front. There are several companies and technical interviewers I know who even make this a simple binary: if they're in a suit, they can't code. Or they're in the wrong place for their project manager interview. Tech organizations discriminate strongly not just against wearing suits but also against people who could be described as "suits." They assume you're there to look good instead of think good.

Personally, I think that wearing dresses and skirts causes problems for women in technical job interviews. This isn't something people process on a conscious level. It's something I've learned over years of watching how people react to women in dresses when they show up for a tech interview. If you start looking around for an outlet or an Ethernet port and find one under a desk, and one of your future male colleagues says, "Here, you shouldn't be crawling around under there dressed like that. Let me help you," you've sent an unfortunate message without realizing it. There are a lot of people who disagree with me on this one. Some women find that skirts are more comfortable for them, and some women think that they shouldn't be prevented from wearing what they want to an interview. To the first group, I say that the interview process isn't about being perfectly comfortable; it's artificial, and it's about appearing as a good potential member of a team. To the second group, I agree with you. No one is going to stop you from wearing what you want to any job interview.

For jewelry, as long as this is a technical job where you'll be a programmer and not a manager, no one cares how many piercings you have. If your jewelry is noisy or tempts you to fidget with it, swap it out for something quieter. If you have more than, say, ten piercings, you might find it difficult to move up in management, but I've never been witness to or heard of anyone not getting a technical job within the last ten years because they had a few facial piercings.

On religious jewelry and dress: I cannot think of an instance where a Sikh wearing a turban, a Russian Orthodox woman wearing a scarf, or a Muslim wearing the hijab could cause a problem, so long as your clothing does not create a hazard. You will unfortunately face whatever discrimination is directed toward your religion, but your dress itself won't be the issue. As a leader, I try to foster an environment in which people of all faiths feel comfortable, so I don't wear highly noticeable religious jewelry. I've seen plenty of people wearing Stars of David, crosses, crescents, and other religious insignia that seem appropriate and don't bother others. I don't think a necklace or small symbol is inappropriate. I am Catholic, and I have specifically asked several prominent tech leaders not of my faith whether they have any problem with the small medals I wear, and none of them have even noticed them. Most religious jewelry is obscure enough that it serves as in-group identification, not as a big signpost.

Tattoos are fine provided that they are not disruptive or profane. If you have disturbing or explicit tattoos, cover them up and expect to keep them covered while you work. I personally don't care if people have religious or political tattoos so long as they are not discriminatory or an incitement to violence, but it could become an issue if you want to be promoted—and you may never realize it was a reason you weren't considered.

As a woman, you cannot win on this one, but my best advice is to not wear heavy makeup. Techies like to think of themselves as serious-minded folk, and heavy makeup can cause some cognitive dissonance. You could be taken for a marketer or receptionist, and no one will realize why they made that assumption. Unfortunately, women who wear at least some makeup are generally seen as more professional and polished than women who do not. Though in my opinion it matters less in a technical interview, it does help to wear lip gloss and powder at least. I know it's not fair or right; I'm telling you what I see succeed and what many others who've done research on professional women have found.

Fragrance: don't. Even scented deodorant may cause problems, and many offices have rules barring scents now.

If you have never had acrylic nails or nail extensions before, this is not the time to get them. I varnish my nails with LED-cured shellac, which keeps them always looking perfect and shiny. People will be staring at your hands as you type, and you'll want your hands to appear neat and well-groomed without fumbling with new nail lengths. This is another lesson I learned the hard way, and one of the reasons I stopped wearing acrylics and gel nails.

The number one mistake I see women make with their hair is not tying it back and then fiddling with it during the interview. Get your hair out of your face. Make sure that your ears are visible (meaning that your whole face is visible) and that if you flip your head forward, no hair will flop over your face. A neat ponytail or bun, braids, cornrows, dreads, or pinned-back natural hair is fine. If you're in systems administration or infosec, a mohawk might even get you extra credit. See also: *The Girl with the Dragon Tattoo*. Don't opt for a messy updo or elaborate hairstyles with lots of curls. Feel free to rock green or fuchsia hair unless you're interviewing for senior technical management.

Wear comfortable shoes that make you as tall as possible—salary increases with height. I'm pretty tall already, but if you're shorter, consider wearing comfortable shoes that add a few inches to your height, such as platform tennis shoes or blocky black leather shoes. You may be walking miles during this interview, especially if you have interviews in different buildings on a tech company campus, and having bleeding feet from high heels won't help your image or your concentration.

Wear everything you are going to wear to the interview a week before. Take your outfit out to the coffee shop, the office, a restaurant, a networking event, or a party. You need to know whether the straps will slip, the socks will bunch, your hair will fall down, or your shoes will pinch. If you pick at your clothes and can't seem to get comfortable, your interviewers won't attribute it to a poor fashion choice—they'll subconsciously process your fidgeting as nervousness. Choose comfort over fashion. When in doubt and starting from scratch, wear a black cardigan over a white blouse and charcoal slacks with plain black shoes and a low ponytail or pinned-back hair.

THE DIFFERENT PARTS OF A TECH INTERVIEW

Multipart interviews are often conducted under the name "tech interview." Here are some of the different kinds of interviews that can happen during an interview round and some of the ways that women might need to think a little differently.

Whiteboarding

This is the interview you've been training for. There are lots of books and resources out there to help you prepare for this portion of the interview process in depth. *Cracking the Coding Interview* by Gayle Laakmann McDowell is the biggest seller. I heartily recommend Michael Reinhardt's *Inside the Tech Interview*. I wrote one of the chapters, and it's a great book full of solid advice. Because everyone will be tested on different technologies, I can't cover exactly what you should do during the interview, but I can tell you some behaviors that have worked well for me and may for you too. First, relax and smile. Keep your voice calm, and take long, deep breaths throughout the process. You'll be asked to write code on a whiteboard with no access to a computer, and this is often the pass or fail portion of the interview. Basically, they're trying to find out how you think and if you actually know what you said you know on your résumé. If you have told them that you have five years of experience in Java and you cannot write even a single line of Java on the board to print a string, this is where they end the process. Because I came into tech through the side door, I actually didn't know that I'd have to write code on a whiteboard the first time I did a tech interview. I freaked out internally but stayed calm and wrote some HTML and CSS to display a centered image, which convinced them that

I knew enough to at least get started. Questions are often that simple. That's all you're trying to do here. If you haven't been through a whiteboard interview before and you're preparing for an interview at your dream job, I highly encourage you to practice first. Get the books, find a tech interview coach, and do at least one or two sessions where you get some critique on your code and your responses to questions. If you get a real jerk of a tech interviewer, they might try telling you that you're wrong when you're not just to see how you handle conflict. This is not common, but it's not unheard of, either. It also seems to happen regardless of gender, weirdly enough. I think that what interviewers think they're testing for is whether coders can defend themselves and correct the interviewers (without blowing up in anger or becoming difficult). As I mentioned before, when faced with the conflict-reduction techniques that many women use, an interviewer can be completely thrown off guard and think that the woman cannot stand up for herself. You need to work out calm responses to this situation in advance with a good coach.

The whiteboard portion of the interview is also the one that is most likely to trigger a panic or fight-or-flight response in you. If that happens, turn to face the whiteboard so the interviewer cannot see your face. Say "Just give me a second. I'm going to silently think through this for a bit." Quietly exhale all the way. Hold the exhale for a four-count. Inhale for a four-count. Hold the inhale for a four-count. Exhale for a four-count. Hold the exhale, and repeat this process four times, pressing your toes hard into the ground on the inhale and releasing your toes on the exhale. It's not possible for your body to process the brain chemicals related to panic and flight while you're breathing calmly and squeezing your toes. Practice it now, and you'll have a great tool to use if you start to get very nervous. (Thanks to Michael Reinhardt for parts of this technique, which I have actually used in interviews before to excellent effect.)

Here's the strategy I've developed, use now, and teach to others for whiteboarding. I divide the board in thirds in my mind and draw a vertical line one-third of the way from the left-hand side. Then I divide that third of the board into a top, middle, and bottom section in my mind, and draw a line a third of the way from the top to the previous line.

Repeat back the exact question the interviewer asks you. Write that question in the top left box. Ask if the interviewer would like

| The problem to solve | Code |
| Pseudocode | |

to see you write out the steps in pseudocode in the lower left-hand box. This is a trick question; no interviewer ever says no to seeing you show your work. Write out the pseudocode for your answer in that box. Then use this trick: ask the interviewer "If I execute this pseudocode for you, will that answer this question?" while pointing to the question that you wrote down above. This stops them from several of the nastier tricks they can pull and forces them to think through your work too. You'll secretly learn several interesting things at this point, like whether the interviewer can solve the problem set for you or was intending to trick you in some way. See, if you execute the pseudocode on the board in the big box, you have fulfilled the task set for you, by the interviewer's own agreement. The interviewer may then ask you to solve more problems, and you'll be off and running with a victory. Now do what Douglas Adams says, and don't panic. You'll do wonderfully!

The Team Get-Together

You'll often be asked to join the team for a lunch or informal get-together to see how you mix with them. Don't let the presence of stale pizza confuse you—you are indeed still being interviewed. This is where you join in the chatter but try not to become the center of attention. It is the best possible place to find out if you'll like working for this company. Don't waste it by worrying about what they think of you—instead, figure out whether you like the team's energy, the environment, the decor, the space, and the company's look and feel. You'll be spending a lot of time here, after all. Focusing on this will keep you from being self-conscious and will give you more data as you decide whether to take the job or not.

The Quick Drop-In to the CEO
or Division Head's Office

If you didn't have a meeting with a division head or CEO on your interview round agenda but are called in to meet with one, congratulations! Your interviewers are interested in you, and you're being rushed ahead in the process to the final OK from the person who's handling the budget to hire you. Just say hello and don't worry too much about this person, who is likely only eyeballing you to see if you can be client facing. This is code for "can talk to other humans without embarrassing the company." If you don't spit food on the CEO, you're probably just fine.

The Follow-Up

Within a matter of ten to thirty minutes after getting out of the round of interviews, send an email to the people you interviewed with. Tell them you had a great time, you look forward to hearing from them, and you were grateful for the opportunity. Do not wait to send a thank-you card through snail mail, since the decision-making process will likely happen within twenty-four hours. In reality, they decided almost instantly upon meeting you whether you'd be hired (whether or not they realized it), but the company itself will likely make the institutional and budgetary decision within twenty-four hours.

WHEN TO REFUSE TASKS AND WHEN TO END THE INTERVIEW

When You're Asked to Do a Task That Is Gendered

Some strange things can come up during tech interviews that no one can prepare you for in college. I remember a time that I was doing a technical interview in Java for a company in downtown Seattle. I did a reasonably decent job on the interview until we came to a pair programming exercise that they'd clearly done with lots of other developers. They had an interview script and performances by other developers to which they wanted to compare me. One developer sat down next to me and pulled out his notes. "OK," he said. "Write a single bowling game."

"Huh?" I said, intelligently.

"Write up a single frame in bowling, with the ability to iterate to ten frames," he said, thinking I hadn't heard him.

"OK, I'm happy to give it a shot. Can you explain what you mean by a game of bowling? And what's a frame?"

It had never occurred to my interviewer that someone interviewing for the job he was hiring for wouldn't know the scoring system for bowling. They spent thirty minutes explaining what they meant by "write a simulation of bowling." By the time I understood what they wanted to see me do, the interview was over. I had written four lines of code and had no idea what I was doing. Needless to say, I didn't get the job.

By choosing subject material for test questions that is stereotypically known by one gender and not the other, the company may be kneecapping itself when it comes to interviewing more diverse candidates. How do you handle this when you're the candidate interviewing? Acknowledge instantly that bowling may be a fun game but that you're not aware enough of the rules to be able to perform favorably in the time you have been given. This is the polite way to tell them that they've given you a task that isn't appropriate or suited to your skill set without actually calling them blithering idiots. This is what I should have done when I was asked, but I was too afraid to do it. Also, offer some alternatives. I would have been quite capable of simulating football or basketball. I actually asked them if I could simulate a field goal in American football instead, but they denied me the chance, saying they wanted to compare me to the other developers they'd had do the test. I would not be surprised if bowling was a big part of the culture there. I would be very surprised if they had more than a few women programmers at that company. I'd be utterly shocked to learn that they had any senior women technologists, especially any in charge of interviewing.

Update: I've been telling that story about the bowling simulation for several years, and just a few weeks ago, I met someone who works there. I avidly inquired as to whether the company still did the bowling simulation, and this person said yes. I asked them how many women programmers were there, and they said they weren't sure, but hadn't seen any in a long time—and that they didn't know of any senior technical women in the company at all. This is a sign of a company that not only has a problem, but doesn't care.

When to Get the Hell Out of There

Sometimes, men will open doors for you and offer to pay for lunch. If they're interviewing you, they should be paying for lunch anyway—but I'll never forget when the man interviewing me over lunch at a café next to the company's offices said, "A gentleman wouldn't let a lady pay," while swiping the bill from me as if we were on a date. He'd just gotten done quizzing me on how well I'd "handle the masculine energy" on the team if he hired me as the lead dev. While walking out he rushed to the door to open it for me with a sweeping gesture. To this day I'm not sure if he was hoping to get my number, but that company certainly lost out when I turned down that job before even waiting to hear back from them (and told every woman I know to avoid the place). There is no "handling" that behavior. Turn down the job, especially if the person interviewing you is the one for whom you'll be working.

If you have a more serious problem during any interview, get out and to a safe place. It's extremely rare but not unheard of for women to face serious sexual harassment during the tech interview process, and they can be so shocked that they don't know how to cope. Do whatever you need to do to feel safe. Then, if you choose to do so, find someone who can assist you. If you don't know anyone, contact me on Twitter or at my email address (which is always easy to find and will be on my personal website), and I'll confidentially help you find a mentoring group, a coach, someone to listen, and resources to help you.

THE ULTIMATE SECRET TO JOB INTERVIEWS

I had a job once that was very prestigious. I was seen as being both lucky and skilled to have the position, and lots of people were very jealous of me. When my husband dropped me off in the morning, he built in ten extra minutes so I could sob because I didn't want to set foot onto the parking lot pavement. I needed three minutes to cry, three minutes to fix my mascara, and four minutes to get hugs and remember how huge my paycheck would be. I will never ever do a job under those working conditions again under any circumstances that don't involve actually sleeping on the street. If I'd really understood what I was getting myself into, I would have never taken that offer.

Here's the punch line: You're interviewing them too.

Trust me, this company wants you to be thrilled about the opportunity to work there and not to have taken the job because it was the best salary offer you could get. It's expensive to replace and hire workers, and if you self-select to not work there, the head bean counter and all the people whose time you didn't waste are quite glad you did so. So, let's talk about how to mindfully interview the company as much as they're interviewing you.

Interviews are a totally artificial process. I'm not the first person to compare them to dating, and I'm going to continue the analogy. The goal of both a first interview and first date is to get to the second. You need to practice both dating and interviewing to be good at them, and sometimes that involves going out and having a nice time with people and companies that you don't have any intention of continuing on with. They're deliberately pressure-filled situations to evaluate you as close to your real self as possible. Your best option is to find a character and a pattern that you can adopt that is really you but is also artificially constructed enough that you won't have your feelings hurt if you're rejected. You can let your guard down more later, as the relationship progresses.

Here's where the analogy breaks down. The interviewee is assumed to be grateful for any offer and willing to do anything to get the job, and it's solely the company's decision about whether the interviewee will be working there. If this were dating, it would be like dating Clark Gable (rroowww). It might be nice to imagine dating a star, but in real life there should be two people equally and enthusiastically consenting to a relationship dyad, not one person dictating and the other person acquiescing.

In interviewing you're almost never interviewing with the people you'll actually be working with. They've been selected for their ability to figure out if you'll be a good fit for the company's culture, and they almost never really care about whether your team will like you. You're trying to get past them as a gatekeeper to the people you actually want to learn about: your potential team. That's a good thing: it gives you the chance to poke around and kick the tires of the culture. Ultimately, if you realize that the company you're interviewing at will hold who and what you are against you, don't work there. Go work somewhere else where people will treat you with respect. Even ten years ago this might not have been true, but there are too many companies out there that want you (yes, YOU) to come and help them find different ways of thinking and will appreciate and reward you for your unique perspective and skills.

THREE-STEP PROCESS

anewaiossmtbarynodwneigftwihonamivatonii.oc

<TYPES OF TECH JOBS and SALARY NEGOTIATIONS>

FULL-TIME, CONTINGENT STAFF, VENDING, TEMPING, AND A 1099

In the tech world, the difference between full-time employment and contract employment is a dirty (but open) secret.

The most familiar class of technical employee is an FTE (full-time equivalent) or W-2 employee at a company, meaning that the job usually comes with a salary, benefits, stock options, and a very small measure of job security. The other class is a 1099 employee (contractor or contingent staff), meaning that the person is usually paid hourly, has no benefits, and is not truly part of the company. Neither of these positions is inherently better than the other, and your choice about which to do is up to you. "W-2" and "1099" refer to the US Internal Revenue Service paperwork you fill out to accept each position; a 1099 form is the tax form for an independent contractor and a W-2 is the tax form for a permanent employee at the company in question.

Here's the real information most people don't tell you about what each position means. First, if you are going to be hired by a company as a full-time employee with benefits, you'll likely be contacted by or speak to an internal recruiter. In general, an internal recruiter is someone hired by BigTechCorp to find and recruit technical talent to work as FTE employees at BigTechCorp. If you're a contractor, you'll likely be contacted by an independent recruiting or vendor agency to work directly for it on contract(s) to another company. A vendor position means that an agency would hire you full time, then loan you out to a tech company, such as Microsoft, Amazon, or Google, to work for them on-site. You'd be a full-time W-2 employee of the vendor agency, rather than an employee of the tech company itself. There are variations on these two kinds of employment, but these are the two big classes. Interestingly, we still call a W-2 employee of XYZ Staffing Agency working at BigTechCorp a contractor, even though they're technically a full-time employee at XYZ.

The real difference: FTE employees are paid less, have some job security, are part of the company culture, and work longer hours. Contractors have zero job security, are paid approximately 40 to 100 percent more than FTEs, are often excluded from company culture and goodies, and can never be legally forced to work unpaid overtime. Note that this difference is only for highly skilled tech workers such as programmers or test engineers. If you're support or administrative staff for a tech company, such as a driver, cafeteria worker, janitor, or other nontechnical employee, none of this applies, and there is increasing attention being paid to the poor working conditions of many contractors in Silicon Valley who perform support tasks like shuttle driving or answering phones. As a contract programmer or tech worker, you are paid more—often a lot more—but you have the same amount of job security that a contract shuttle driver has. None.

Your choice of which kind of employment to take is (mostly) up to you. Personally, I have enjoyed contracting because I like projects and jobs with understandable goals and a clear definition of success, and I like never working unpaid overtime for a company in which I have no personal stake. Many tech companies have a culture of expecting hundred-plus-hour work weeks on occasion or even regularly, and I saw a lot of resentment on the part of salaried employees at the real pay they were receiving. I've even been told by a few employees at some of the larger companies that if they added up their real hours and divided their pay by that number, they'd be better off and happier asking "Do you want fries with that?" On the other hand, the fat stock options and benefits provided to FTE employees as well as being accepted inside a culture and working toward the common long-term goals of a company can provide amazing incentives to people who like much more stability. Still, the tech world seems to be trending toward more contracting and remote work as people grow more specialized in their tech skills and remote working tools improve.

Over the course of this book, you'll read about a few absolutely nonnegotiable positions I have when it comes to accepting employment, even at the cost of not being paid for a while. One of them involves nondisclosure agreements from vendor agencies. Let me tell you why.

A friend recently asked me to pass along information about a job opening for a project manager position at a local tech company. The tech company pays the agency an hourly rate, called the client bill rate. You, the worker, have your own hourly rate with the agency. Here's the tricky part: the vendor agency is under no obligation to tell you how much their client bill rate is. If you've signed a nondisclosure agreement with your agency and the on-site company, you will have no idea what your time is actually worth.

In general, tech client bill rates are at least $70 an hour in 2015 US dollars. A contractor on a 1099 with a bill rate of $70 an hour would receive the full amount and then pay state and federal employment taxes and costs (covered by your employer in a W-2 situation and often coming as a total surprise to the independent contractor during their first tax year)—perhaps 30 percent of the total—leaving them with $49 per hour before their own taxes, and then approximately $35 per hour as take-home pay (which is a common amount for a Seattle web developer with starting skills and under one year of experience). However, when a contractor operates through a vendor agency, she becomes a vendor and is instead issued a W-2 paycheck based not on her client bill rate but on her hourly wages with the agency.

Think of it this way: a fair bill rate for a senior developer with extremely specialized skills and fifteen years of experience might be $250 per hour. Taking $75 an hour of that is a 30 percent charge and results in $175 per hour for this highly skilled worker who is now thrilled and happy with the agency. But what actually happens most of the time is something like this: the agency tells the dev that the dev will be paid $80 per hour, and then the agency pockets the remaining $170 as a 68 percent charge. In fact, agency recruiters are incentivized to maximize the difference between the client bill rate and the vendor hourly rate—because that's where bonuses on their commissions come in. Consider that along with the nondisclosure agreement, and you should be realizing now in a way you never did before that if you are working for a vendor agency that does not disclose their client bill rate, you are not your recruiter's client or partner. You're their product.

Contracting is how the tech industry gets around labor laws. Now, because tech workers are paid so much, there is little public outrage on their behalf when labor laws are skirted, ignored, or outright violated. This is a problem. Contracting means that the tech company can work contractors for eighty hours a week or more with total impunity, so long as they pay the agency for the vendors' time. Then the vendor agency merely pays whatever hourly wage they have settled on with the vendor. This system, which is manipulative in its own right, is also abused by many companies, who ask contractors to do work off the books or off-site to "make sure this contract stays open at renewal time" or ask them to double their hours one week and work nothing the next, while being paid as if they were working a regular amount on a weekly basis.

To make matters worse, many major companies with brand-name recognition work with only a few "preferred vendor agencies," meaning that to take a contract position at a major company and get a feather in your cap, you must agree to work for a preferred agency and risk not knowing your true value to the company. One of my first positions at a major brand-name tech company was as a lead web developer on contract with a vendor agency. This big tech company had a great deal of money after laying off many full-time staff and replacing them with contractors who did not have to be paid benefits. Many of the contractors had previously been full-time employees of the company in question. I cannot reveal my exact rate, but let us assume that I was paid between $40 and $45 per hour. I found out later that my time was being billed to the company at between $110 and $140. It's very common for people with no expertise in negotiation to take the first rate offered to them, leading to an even lower rate for women and minorities than they would have had—and this difference is exacerbated by the conspiracy of secrecy around their actual value. When told that they're not worth a higher rate, women and minorities tend to believe it and accept the amount offered—and while a company could never tell full-time employees that they're not worth the amount they ask for, a vendor agency can do so with total impunity because they're negotiating on behalf of two parties—themselves and their client, not you.

That is correct: your eyes do not deceive you. The company doing nothing more than signing my paperwork as a preferred vendor agency and passing along my employment taxes to the state (about $15 an hour, at my bill rate) was making two and a half times what I was. I received no benefits, no health care, no paid time off, and no overtime extra pay—only the money I was paid hourly.

Tech is actually a very small world, and the existence of blacklists for tech workers who have caused problems in their contracts is real. If you're put on "the list" at a major tech company, you can expect that some other tech companies will refuse to consider you for employment. Standing up for yourself when it comes to inequity, workplace problems, or discrimination can be similar to pursuing a discrimination suit at a major law firm—you can absolutely expect that you will never be hired to work for a large firm again. You may end up with only one option: to start your own firm and declare victory. There's a good reason that top-level minority and female contractors leave high-paying contract gigs to build their own startups and companies. When you work on-site at a tech company but are not employed by that tech company, any discrimination or harassment issues you may face are your tough luck. You don't actually work for that company, so you can only sue your vendor agency if you have issues—and why would you do that? You weren't harassed or discriminated against by your direct superior, so how do you prove a hostile work environment in a company you don't technically work for?

Here's the punch line: I never negotiated my pay with the large tech company I worked for. In that first position, I was treated well by people who themselves had no idea what my bill rate and hourly wage were. I had to negotiate with the vendor agency for my wages. As a result, the vendor agency was incentivized to lie to me with every breath (in fact, I signed paperwork saying that the vendor agency wasn't obligated to be open with me about my bill rate, without necessarily understanding that this meant they could and would lie outright to me about my worth). I was told "This is the way it is if you want that position at XXX Co." I had no reason to doubt that, because I didn't yet know of the existence of full-disclosure vendor agencies.

Let's be clear: vendor agencies serve a great purpose. In tech, investing in an employee is time consuming and resource intensive. If you become an employee at a tech company, it's likely that the company sees a future for you there with multiple roles and an upward trajectory. However, there are a lot of positions at major tech companies that are by nature temporary. If a company has a project that must be executed in Python to work with one of its client's interfaces, and it has a bench full of C++ programmers but no one who specializes in Python, it makes sense for the company to hire a contractor for a short-term job. Think of it this way: you don't invite the people who remodel your kitchen to stick around in case you need them again in a few years. They possess a specialized skill that you need on a temporary basis, and you pay them well to come in, do their job, and leave when they're done, without any feeling of long-term obligation to them.

To extend the analogy, however, imagine that you have hired a construction firm that sends a three-person crew to your house, and you discover that though you are paying the company for the hours that crew spends in your home at the rate of $60 per hour per person, each of the workers make only $11 per hour—the current minimum wage in Seattle. Worse, they have no idea how much you are paying for their time, can be fired and blacklisted for asking, and cannot share their wage information with any of their colleagues.

All of a sudden, your conscience starts to twinge. Why is it that the best construction business in town won't share its rates with its own employees? Why not be honest about what it is paying for these services? Doing so doesn't change the amount itself. All it does is empower workers to choose an agency that treats them with respect and transparency.

This is why I do not pass along information on jobs from vendor and contracting agencies that will not disclose their client bill rate. I will not work for one, and I strongly encourage you to never do so, either. If you're a vendor agency, it is understandable and appropriate to charge anywhere between 15 and 40 percent of the client bill rate for your services. After all, you're handling employment taxes, W-2s, accounting, paperwork, direct deposit, and possibly benefits as desired by either the employee or agency. You should be making a good profit on your service to both parties. However, taking

85 percent of the client bill rate and leaving scraps for the actual worker, all the while hiding behind a nondisclosure agreement, is morally indefensible, no matter how legal the agreement you signed with a clueless contractor.

Considering the tenuous nature of contracting, why do I still enjoy it and encourage you to think about it? I've sat next to someone making $48 per hour, assuming a forty-hour workweek, as a FTE employee, and I was paid double for the same job. Also, I actually did work forty hours a week—and he worked seventy as a salaried employee ineligible for overtime. You do the math.

SALARY NEGOTIATION: MINUTE ZERO IN THE GENDER PAY GAP

Now that you understand better the consequences of choosing contracting or FTE work, let's have a chat about minute zero in the gender pay gap—the moment in your life that you have the most power to improve your economic condition and conquer the 21 percent Lady Tax.

Just the other day, I was coaching a woman through a salary negotiation. No matter how many times I told her that she was being moved through the interview process with indecent haste, that the company clearly wanted her, that her skill set and rarity in the job market made her much more valuable than what she was being offered, and that in days she could have multiple competing offers with a big pay bump, she chose to believe the negotiator's claim that they couldn't pay more than the somewhat-below-averagerate she was offered. She was afraid that if she bargained, she'd be seen as a bitch and a user by her teammates. She took the offer.

I know how hard salary negotiation is. Men who see the salary gap between their female and male hires ask me in bewildered tones "Why didn't she just negotiate harder?" because they don't understand that for women, there is a serious economic and social penalty for not being liked. We have the statistics and research behind this fact: women's likability decreases with their success, while men's likability increases with their success. Likability is not a trivial or meaningless concept; if a woman is disliked, her economic status is directly affected.

We need to provide answers to problems like this one: "The hiring manager said he couldn't offer me any more salary, so I took the job—then found out that everyone else had negotiated higher salaries, and I'm being paid 20 percent less than the others. How do I get more money?"

Sometimes a company culture of secrecy around pay leads to huge pay disparities. I remember being in a room with a male hiring manager who barely looked me in the eyes, droned company policy at me, and didn't look up from his paperwork until he stated the lowball offer he'd been told to give me. I gave him the response I'll teach you about below: "That's a great place to start!" For the first time, he really noticed there was another human in the room, and somewhat taken aback, he politely told me that he didn't usually get those sorts of responses (the unspoken subtext was "from women"), but that he'd get back to me. A day later, I had an offer that was 10 percent better than I'd even hoped for.

I'm a big believer in the 80/20 rule (also known as Pareto optimality for my fellow academics). This rule is commonly used to mean that you can invent a usable solution for most problems rapidly, and that there are diminishing returns on perfection. If you can solve 80 percent of the problem in five minutes rather than 100 percent of the problem in six months, choose the first option and constantly iterate for better. You'll take a giant leap toward your goal salary just by remembering these four common negotiating tactics used by recruiters and hiring managers, and preparing a script in advance to counter them. Remember that you'll be flustered, stressed, and trying to make your new company happy, and in the moment, if you don't have a script to follow, you'll give in and try to make others happy rather than yourself.

TACTIC 1: *"We'll need you to tell us what you'd expect as a salary."*

Hell no, they don't. They want you to prove you're a team player by naming a low number so that you'll be guaranteed to get the job. Do not name a number first. I repeat: *Do not name a number first. No naming of numbers first.* Here's your script: "The salary you offer me tells me a lot about this company, and I think it's really important for me to have that information so I can compare you with my other offers. [I don't care if your gee-paw in Oklahoma has offered you $50 to clean out the garage; that's still another job offer, and everyone has a few of those. It's none of the negotiator's business whether you'll accept those other offers or not.] I'm happy to give you some time; why don't I follow up with you tomorrow if I haven't heard your offer by then? I know it can take some time to get the i's dotted!" You can only pull this off if you mean it and you're being cheerful, helpful, and totally honest with them. It's one of the few moves that tells them that you're in demand and happy to give them time but absolutely unwilling to make the first offer. You will lose money in every situation where you name the number first. While there's tons of math and analyses behind that statement, here's the simple logic. It is impossible for you to name the correct number. You will either name a number that is higher than theirs, casting you in the role of the unreasonable person, or name a number that is lower, meaning you'll be underpaid the entire time you're at that company. Always be the person to respond to an offer so that you can follow my next piece of advice.

TACTIC 2: *Never, ever say yes to the first offer.*

I'll say it again. This moment—the moment where they're offering you a salary that's bigger than your college work-study self could ever have imagined—is minute zero in the gender pay gap.

There is a very gendered response to this moment. Men assume all salaries are negotiable and don't say yes to the first offer (yes, I know I'm summarizing by gender, but it's borne out by multiple deep statistical and quantitative studies on how men and women negotiate or do not). Women say thank you. Don't do it. Here's your script: "That's a great place to start!"

I'm not going to give detailed instructions here because this moment is a very, very difficult point for many people—not just women but men as well can have trouble saying no to the first offer. I want you to believe with every ounce of your being that the person talking to you wants you to work for them much, much more than you want to work for them. Here's why: it's true. It costs in excess of $30,000 to find and recruit a single top developer, put them through interview rounds, and do onsite evaluations, and I promise you right now: they're *exhausted*. It's still hugely expensive to recruit and hire even for nontechnical roles—around $18,000 for a project manager in the Seattle area (according to my local top recruiting sources behind closed doors and over martinis). They don't want you to leave the room. There's no one standing outside their door waiting to jump into the hot seat you just vacated. They'll have weeks of work ahead of them to get another candidate to the same point in interviews and negotiations that you're at right now. If they can spend an hour or so with you adding some benefits and a pay bump to your contract, they absolutely will, and with a sigh of relief.

If you've given too much and/or you named a number first, which they accepted, you can still use the responses above when negotiating intangibles in Tactic 3.

So how do you add some intangible benefits or a pay bump to your salary while still being a team player? Here's the next tactic.

TACTIC 3: *"This salary is not negotiable."*

This line is often used by companies who have a salary band that is based on some kind of "quantifiable" metric for parsing résumés. Have a master's degree? Get a 5 percent pay bump. Have a CISSP? Get a 5 percent pay bump. Only a bachelor's degree? Bottom of the salary band.

First, bullcrap. As the positively magnificent Baroness Rodmilla de Ghent says in *Ever After* to Cinderella, "Nothing's final until you're dead, and even then, I'm *sure* God negotiates." (I may have a hard time telling villainess from heroine in any movie where Anjelica Huston chews scenery.) Just because there's no getting around the salary band doesn't mean they don't want you on board.

Second, the person you're negotiating with is almost certainly unconnected with the team. You'll be negotiating with a professional salary negotiator in human resources, and their job is to make you doubt yourself and your value just enough that you'll take the first offer, gratefully. You don't realize it, but they're not reporting back to your team and future manager to tell them that you're a hard case in negotiations; most of the time, your team and manager won't even know what you're being paid. That was the case with the woman I told you about at the beginning of this chapter. I'm still working on a way to effectively get women to understand their value, and I feel like it was a failure on my part that I didn't say the right things to make her believe in herself enough to say what I'll teach you next.

Third, here's your script: "That's a great place to start! I understand that you cannot go outside the salary band, so let's work on finding other ways to get your offer commensurate with my others, because I love this company and I really want to find a way to work here. What can you do in the way of stock options and tele-commuting? If you can contractually add two days a week where I don't have to fight Seattle traffic, we're all winners!"

Here's what's happening here: it's the same tactic as before about being a team player, dressed up in "company policy." It's a little more difficult to get around, but I just shared the way you can do so. To use this response effectively, you need to really understand the value of the offer they're making you and of what else they can offer. I'll put up with a lot in a company that doesn't make me leave my house to work with them, because in the Seattle area, traffic is so bad that most people consider any commute that has a bridge in it to be profoundly difficult to manage day to day (and let's not even speak of the two-hour seven-mile commute from Redmond to Seattle across one bridge). This isn't a random complaint—I get twenty to twenty-five hours of my life back (and hugely decreased associated costs like food and transportation) each week if I work remotely rather than commuting, and you should seriously consider that as an option for getting around salary band requirements.

Stock options are another possibility, but negotiating for equity and vested options is very complex, and I can't give you general rules for it; each situation will be different. In a salary band situation, you'll be trying hard to get other benefits that equate to real cash for you without causing the other person to break company policy. Do you walk or bike to work? Is there a paid parking pass benefit? Ask them to instead give you a transit pass or a velodrome membership (this one works like gangbusters in any company with pretensions of being green or socially conscious). Is there a paid gym membership you know you won't use? Ask for a childcare credit in that same amount. That's how you get around the salary band. (Unless it's a government or academic job. There's no negotiating there; take it or leave it.)

TACTIC 4: *"This is the average market salary rate for people with your job description, so that's why we're offering it."*

They may justify it with a reference to Salary.com or Glassdoor .com. It's hard to say no to this; we as humans are strongly trained to believe in fairness, and women are socialized to value being seen as team players. This negotiator is using a very common and manipulative tactic where you have to justify being unfair to others to get what you want.

Instead, try this: "I'm here and interested in this job because I think your company is extraordinary, not average. I don't think you want to fill this company with average developers, and I don't think you'd be offering me this opportunity if you did. Glassdoor has a salary for someone of my abilities and training at [number that is at least 20 percent more than what they cited you]. Is that a little closer to what the amazing people I've met so far have started at?"

Anytime someone tries to convince you that you should take an "average" salary, turn the tables on them by forcing them either to say out loud that you're average or to backtrack and offer you more.

Practice with a partner right now. You need to know how it feels to speak each of these lines before you're in a pressure-filled situation. It's going to be very, very hard to say no to someone asking you to say yes to a job you want. Humans are built to cooperate with each other, and saying no to someone offering you money will be a difficult exercise for you. Work through it in advance to make sure you never say no. Think of it this way: you're offering a better option that can make both sides happier and helping yourself in the process.

"Diplomacy is the art of letting someone else have your way."
—DANIELE VARE

WATCH OUT DURING NEGOTIATIONS

You're Not Guinevere

Frequently there are short trial periods where you're still negotiating your work, signing paperwork, and being brought onboard, and this is one situation you may discover during your first few weeks on the job. It's extraordinarily common for women developers to face it and to not realize that they cannot fix it.

Management types will often view Developer Land as a snake pit of boyish behavior, sexist jokes, inappropriate high jinks, and basement-dwelling mouth breathers. Usually when someone higher up realizes that there are no women engineers on staff and that every coder they have is a walking potential HR disaster, this same someone decides that hiring women engineers is a priority in order to use the "civilizing effect that women have on men." You might be the first woman hired into a company, team, or department. If you are, no matter how many times you're assured that you're being hired for your skill set, chances are that the hiring managers breathed a sigh of relief that you're a good fit for the job. Hiring managers understand that women are underrepresented in tech, and they do in general want to see you aboard. They might have wanted to see diversity in their company for other reasons than you think, however. Be wary of a situation where you're the first woman on the team and you get the spoken or unspoken message that they're glad to have you because they expect you to make the team grow up and act like professionals.

There's a serious problem with this assumption. In reality, one or two women will not civilize a team of brogrammers. It is management's job to not hire jackasses. It is not the job of the new web developer who also happens to identify as female to civilize them.

In addition, those newly hired women will rarely have any power, and a hiring manager who initially thought that it was a good idea to hire male coders who have sexist jokes on their T-shirts isn't likely to be sympathetic to complaints (even if the manager was clearly and specifically told to hire women).

The other problem with the assumption that women will civilize a dev team is that it presumes that women who want to be developers are women who have low, sweet voices, courteous shyness, and a Guinevere complex, and require coats to be thrown on puddles. In reality, most women developers are giant nerds who are just as likely if not more so than the men to be outsiders—people who have fought even harder than the men have to shore up their sense of identity and who have no desire whatsoever to change what outsiders to the geek culture might view as immaturity or social inappropriateness. Comic book collecting, an MMORPG habit, action figures, wearing elf ears to conventions, and winning at Star Trek trivia are not signs of immaturity or a lack of social skills in the geek world; they are shibboleths. They display a sense of in-group pride, and as such, they actually constitute some of the soft skills that can help you fit in.

The Difference between Trying and Fronting

There is a big difference between a workplace that has not yet been able to acquire female engineers and is trying to do so and a workplace that is trying to change a culture that actively discourages or even prevents women from joining as engineers.

In the first case, you may be treated with touching and even amusing amounts of courtesy and political correctness. Once I was speaking with an older gentleman who was a VP of engineering. He ended a conference call with me and another woman with "OK, guys, talk to you later. I mean . . . girls. I mean gals. I mean ladies . . . women! Sorry!" We laughed, because there are far worse ways to be treated than overly courteously. Be kind to them and let them off the hook; they're trying. A sense of humor helps here; try saying "Just don't call me late for dinner" or something along those lines. After a while, they'll relax and worry more about how well they're treating you than whether you'll get offended at every little verbal slip. It's easy to see when people are trying hard to be inclusive and caring.

In the second case, you'll hear jokes or comments that have a very different undertone. These are the jackasses who tell blonde jokes or ask what you tell a woman with two black eyes. They'll expect you to laugh them off, because in the other parts of their nerd group, these kinds of jokes are encouraged, or at least not discouraged, by other people in their lives who have little power to change the situation. They're testing to find out how far they can push you and whether you'll put up with sexist humor that has no kindness or irony behind it. An unfortunate part of nerd humor is inappropriate jokes and one-upsmanship with vulgar humor. If you hear this undertone and encounter this situation, especially all throughout the company, either get up or get out. (Get promoted or leave the company.) There is no way to change that situation, and it's going to exhaust and hurt you in the long run—not just professionally but personally.

If you find out after being hired that the perceived reason for your hiring was to make the boys grow up, start looking for a new job. That culture is broken, and you will not fix it. Even on the off chance that you spend hours, days, weeks, or months trying to get the others to behave and you somehow magically do, you've wasted your time on a task that gives you no extra money, takes up your emotional energy, and saps your desire to be in tech. You're doing extra work for no extra pay. You didn't get hired as a cultural development specialist, and you're not contributing to your résumé . . . just your collection of war stories.

THE SYSADMIN
Miah Johnson

When I was a child, my parents introduced me to the mechanical and technical world. My father introduced me to aspects of
mechanical engineering through work on our minibikes, quads, and
snowmobiles. Our garage was filled with tools, and so we ended
up building and fixing all the things. We also spent tons of time
outdoors, camping, fishing, and hunting. I really enjoyed camping
and fishing, but hunting required sitting still in the winter cold for
far too long. Fishing was a similar experience, but at least you were
on a boat on a lake, or sitting on the side of a river in the summer.
The fun part of this was always learning how things worked; taking
things apart and putting them back together was my favorite way
to learn.

My mother worked in human resources and accounting, and
went to school while working full time. She sometimes brought
me into her college classes, and several of them were computer
related. Sometimes she brought home computers from work so
that she could work over the weekend, and I tried to get as much
time playing on them as I could. Even though her "laptop" was
running DOS and had no games installed, I'd usually find a game
in the stack of floppies that was in the case. After reading the
instructions on the floppy label, I was usually able to figure out
how to get into the game, even if I couldn't figure out how to play
the game well.

When I saw the Commodore 64 commercials on TV, I asked my parents over and over for it; I didn't get it, but I always wanted a computer. The closest I got was an Atari 5200, and then a Nintendo. Because we didn't have a computer at home, I joined an after-school program called Computer Club; we used mostly Apple II computers, and played games and printed things. It was super fun, and I was addicted.

Because my mom worked and my dad was often away for military operations, I went to summer camp every year. Sometimes it was the typical YMCA stuff, which was fun, but I was most excited when I was able to get into a computer camp. I remember spending a few weeks at one where we programmed things in BASIC and having the time of my life. When I was thirteen, my mom got an Intel 486 for the house, which I didn't do much with at first apart from playing games, but once I figured out how to work the modem and get on Prodigy, it was all over. I started spending all my waking hours on the computer, figuring out that while Prodigy was expensive on a per-minute basis, I could dial into local computer bulletin board systems (BBSs) and get a similar experience for free.

This evolved into me installing different operating systems on our computer, trying out OS/2, DESQview, and eventually Windows Chicago—a.k.a. Windows 95. Eventually my friend gave me a CD that had Slackware Linux on it, and I installed it on a separate partition after reading the entirety of the Linux Documentation Project. Because I had only a single computer (and no printer), I had to write notes or have an idea of the answer before I booted up Linux. It took me a while to get Linux dialing up to my local BBSs and even longer to figure out how to get PPP (point-to-point protocol) working to dial into our ISP (Internet service provider).

What I loved about computers was that I was able to figure out solutions to problems. The problems themselves could have multiple solutions, but each would be valid. In school, I had to spend a lot of time on showing my work and ensuring that I followed a very specific technique to solve a problem or answer a question.

With computers the answer was somewhat variable, but I had a way to test its validity.

I first got Internet access through a local BBS that had a telnet interface. Because I didn't know much about the Internet and it was all text based, I didn't have a great experience and concentrated mostly on BBSs. Eventually I landed on a BBS that also provided dial-up Internet access for a small fee, but it offered a free trial—for a few hours. Of course, I made a few different accounts and got as much time as I could online, browsing the web with NCSA Mosaic and then Netscape.

I saw the films *Sneakers* and *Hackers* and thought they were cool, so I started searching for sites and groups where I could learn more about hacking and found a site called Hackersclub.com. It wasn't the most hardcore hackers of the Internet; it was mostly kids asking questions about computers and sometimes asking how to hack something. I spent most of my time on their forum answering these questions. I would use all of the search engines (Google didn't exist) and research answers as best I could. After some time, I became well known in the forums and was granted some administrator privileges to remove duplicate or hostile posts.

I ended up skipping school often and hanging out online, learning and chatting. At school, I was a failure of a student, the kind who got a D in every class. The learning environment in school didn't work well for me. The only classes that I really enjoyed were those involving engineering or technology. I took shop and applied technology, and did well, but when it came to math or history, I failed miserably. Unfortunately, because I was not a model student, I was not allowed to take the programming classes. Had I been better in math, this would have been different, but having math as a prerequisite meant programming was never going to happen for me. I was super frustrated with the school system at this point. I felt that it should have been doing a better job at taking students who weren't learning and helping them to do something that they felt was exciting. I felt as if the educators were basically saying that even though this was something I had shown potential in, they didn't care. I had discussions with the teachers from the programming classes and my guidance counselor about how taking those classes might spark my interest in other ones. But in the end, they didn't want to let me in without the prerequisites.

Even though I couldn't take programming classes, I was still really excited about computers. They had grabbed me in a way that nothing else had, and sparked the flame needed for me to dive in and learn everything I could. Just because I couldn't take a class at school didn't mean I couldn't learn about programming. So I taught myself Pascal and C at home in DOS using the Borland compiler tools that I downloaded from some BBS.

Within a few months that BBS site added a Java chat applet called Sneakerchat, and I began to hang out there whenever I had free time. As the site's popularity grew, its administrators started to grow their network. Sneakerchat was replaced with IRC (Internet relay chat), and I spent even more time there getting to know everybody. I skipped a lot of school so I could hang out chatting and made several lifelong friends. I also got to know the site administrators, and they offered me a job. I was still in high school, but they wanted me to at least have my diploma. So I dropped out and got my GED. I ended up moving away from home to Fort Lauderdale, Florida, when I was eighteen to work at my first real job.

I lived and worked in Florida for almost three years. My boss, Pat, taught me much of what he knew about UNIX, Netware, and programming. The co-owner of our company, LuAnn, handled much of the web work and also taught me a lot. Our company supported small businesses. We managed NetWare networks primarily, with some UNIX presence. We also hosted websites and email on servers at our office. I learned a lot about working with people and administering systems. Sometimes I drove hours just to put a floppy disk into a computer and update some software. Few companies had a connection to the Internet, and many were fearful that they might be ripped off if we did any maintenance remotely.

It was just us three at the company, and it felt a lot like having a new family. Pat was like an older brother to me, and LuAnn an older sister. We frequently went out to dinner together and hung out on the weekends. After some time, however, LuAnn left the company, and it was just Pat and me, and the office lost the fun that it used to have.

Around 2000, I was trying to get work at a company that was directly involved with open source software, specifically in the Linux world. I started searching for openings at Red Hat and other companies, seeing if I could somehow get in and learn and contribute even more. Because I had learned so much from open source software, I wanted to give back in any way I could, which for me was working with OSS companies. I wanted to work at a company that wouldn't hoard my work; it should be given away for free! I felt that people who were in similar situations as myself could benefit in some way from what I was doing.

I ended up getting a job at Turbolinux (a friend referred me), so I was in the San Francisco area during the dot-com boom. At Turbolinux I worked on the network security team managing the company firewall, as well as remote office VPNs (virtual private networks). San Francisco was a heady and exciting environment at the time but not very stable. So after undergoing a couple of rounds of layoffs at a couple of jobs (including Penguin Computing, where I was once again working with open source software and doing security work), I decided to get out of California.

After California, I made a bad decision and tried to go back to Florida to see if I could work with Pat again. But the IT industry was not the same in Fort Lauderdale as it was in San Francisco. It was very much a dress-shirt-and-tie work environment that didn't agree with my very purple hair. My time in Florida was super depressing. It was difficult for me to get over the fact that even though I felt that I knew what I was doing and had a record of being a good contributor, my success came down to how I looked and dressed.

I ended up moving to Boston because it was my girlfriend's hometown and I had friends there who told me it was a great place to work. My friends were right, and my new employers loved that I had bright-red hair and was super into computers. I was working part time at the National Resource for Imaging Mass Spectrometry (NRIMS) doing general systems administration on mixed IRIX and Solaris systems. I loved working there, but I generally worked less than twenty hours a week with no benefits, so after my girlfriend told me she was pregnant, I realized I had to get a new job with benefits.

I had become good friends with the office administrator at NRIMS, and she found a position at the Boston Children's Hospital Informatics Program (CHIP) that I would be perfect for. At CHIP I helped professors and doctors with their research programs. I maintained all of their internal services like email and web and provided desktop support. I built Beowulf clusters and supported multi-terabyte disk arrays so that researchers could do analysis on entire genomes. I did work that I felt really good about, because I knew it was helping humanity, not just some worthless startup selling a product nobody cared about.

I didn't enjoy doing desktop support, though, so I worked with the internal IT groups at the hospital to rid myself of that task. I ended up merging my position with the internal research computing group and continuing the UNIX administration aspects of the job while my new coworkers handled desktop support. Being in research computing meant that I helped run systems for research groups other than CHIP, but because I could concentrate on the server-side work, I was able to grow my knowledge. In the research computing group I started experimenting with repeatable installations of servers and making the hospital's internal security policies pass the Center for Internet Security (CIS) standards. Because the CIS list has hundreds of requirements that I had to clear, I started to get into automation. After some time, I had systems that I could install using a Kickstart process, that then fired off CFEngine to do fine-tuning. My CFEngine rules had been constructed so that my boxes passed all the CIS requirements. I was able to demonstrate this to the hospital's internal IT groups by doing a live demo where I installed a new server from scratch during our hour-long meeting.

When the installation was done, I was able to show them working websites and a valid security policy.

I enjoyed working at NRIMS and Boston Children's Hospital because both jobs made me feel good about the work I was doing, and I was able to experiment and learn on my own path. We had requirements about what work needed to be done but rarely about how. The people I worked with were incredibly friendly and smart, and were working on something that benefited all of humanity.

I ended up getting tempted away from that work by the promise of more money and a more stable life for my family, though. A friend visited and told me about the company he was contracting for. He kept trying to convince me to leave Boston and move to Houston to work at Stanford Financial Group. The company's product was diversified investments; instead of stocks, you'd invest in gold coins, commodities, and so forth. In South America and Antigua, the company actually had banks. The key things he kept repeating to me were that I'd be able to buy a house and give my kids a really stable environment to grow up in. I ended up interviewing and taking the offer at SFG. We packed up the family and once again moved cross-country. I was able to buy a house, but sadly it turned out that the company was not 100 percent legit.

I continued doing UNIX administration at my job at SFG. I primarily managed their Oracle database systems, as well as any other UNIX systems, including a printer server based on CUPS that managed payroll for our worldwide employees.

I brought my Kickstart and CFEngine skills in and was able to straighten out many of the issues we had with the database and printer systems, but I struggled to work with the database team. They were not huge fans of my infrastructure and wanted more access and odd one-offs on each server. I remember being really frustrated about my job daily. I felt like no matter how well I designed something, it wasn't good enough. The database team and I frequently struggled to come to an agreement, which made me depressed and angry.

Around this time, the company's internal security team was also starting to hire again, and I decided to switch teams. Before I joined the security group, they had also hired a new manager. I am certain to this day that his job was to fire everybody on that team. I worked in the security group for five months or so until I was fired. It was an impossible job, really. The company, which was spread out all over North and South America, as well as the Caribbean, had horrible security posture. I couldn't get anybody to care that we were being hacked daily, even when we had to reissue all of the ATM cards for Bank of Antigua. It turned out that SFG was a multibillion-dollar Ponzi scheme, and the SEC closed them down within a month of my departure.

Having children to care for as well as a house that I had to maintain meant I had to find more work. I was in an environment similar to South Florida again, and the job market was not that great. I couldn't find anything that wasn't part time or consulting. I was also really struggling with gender dysphoria and had started seeing a therapist and going to transgender meetups. Finally taking control of my transition helped resolve some of my depression. I still had to deal with the stress of finding stable work and making ends meet, but I felt as if I was finally able to live without hiding some aspect of myself. It was hugely freeing and I'm certain that my uplift in feelings helped me get through this very difficult time.

I wanted to get back to a liberal environment and started trying to get a job in California again. We ended up foreclosing on our house and basically abandoning Texas. My wife and children ended up in Michigan with my mom for several months while I tried to get established in San Francisco. After struggling to make ends meet, I was able to get a job at Salesforce in San Francisco, and I decided that with my new job I should just transition. Therapy and life told me it was the right time. Things couldn't really get any worse. My relationship with my wife was in really bad shape, and we were a thousand miles apart. We were both super in debt.

I interviewed at Salesforce before my transition, so after I received my offer letter, I let them know that I was going to be making some changes. My first day at work was fantastic; everybody accepted me, and it seemed as if things were going to get much better.

I think I'm extremely lucky that I was able to transition and work in California. My experience has been mostly positive, and I'm certain that geographic location had a lot to do with that. (I was moving from Texas to California, where there are employment protections for transgender people.) The workplace culture in Silicon Valley is also 100 percent different than in Houston. The problems with tech culture tend to vary based on where you are in the world. I've experienced tech culture in five different states, and so far my favorite experience has been on the West Coast.

After transitioning I did notice that people treated me differently at work. I was and still am unsure if people are doing this because I'm trans or because I'm a woman, or if I'm just imagining it. I thankfully haven't had an issue with workplace harassment. I have had many coworkers who were curious and interested to learn more, and I've ended up telling my story to many coworkers and friends. I think it helps people understand and empathize with transgender issues.

If you're a transgender worker in tech, you can be 100 percent sure that the company you're applying to has exclusions in its health insurance policy and that no one there has any idea how to make it better. Previously I didn't look closely at my health insurance exclusions, and I never worried about it. Now I've been in the position of having to educate HR on the subject multiple times.

I also didn't think I would be the only transgender employee. I've been in that position three times already. If you're the only transgender person, you'll probably be the one educating the company on what needs to change, and that can be extremely draining. Impostor syndrome also seems to go hand in hand with transitioning. You've spent tons of time hiding your true self from the world and are finally letting it out. Suddenly you become less sure of yourself, because the way you interact with the world has changed. (Maybe people can sense my lower confidence, or maybe they want me to go the extra mile because they don't believe in me.) As a result, when applying for work, you have to pay close attention to diversity issues, how your future employer is going to treat you, and if their culture is worth fitting into.

The cost of living in San Francisco made this otherwise positive and exciting time very difficult. My marriage was in shambles, and after much discussion, we decided to get a divorce. I worked at Salesforce for almost three years while I paid off my debts and reestablished myself. While I was there I worked on the technical operations team and managed hundreds of servers. It was stressful, but we had many things scripted to handle some level of automation. It was not anything as powerful as CFEngine or Chef, though, and that eventually took its toll on me.

A good friend of mine told me about a startup he was joining. They were building a competitor to Dropbox. They had nobody doing systems administration for them, and it was totally greenfield. The company was based out of Scottsdale, Arizona, but I worked remotely, and since the company was based on Amazon Web Services (AWS), it didn't matter where I was. CX.com was a great experience, and I jumped right in and designed our systems automation around Chef. Thanks to Chef and AWS, I was able to manage everything easily and learn a ton. I also spent a lot of time in the Chef support IRC channel, and that experience led to me receiving accolades from Chef and becoming well known in that community.

Winning a community contributor award from Chef was one of the most rewarding experiences of my life, but I had no idea it was going to happen. It was a fantastic feeling to hear my name called out and have everybody congratulate me. It makes me feel great to this day, knowing that I helped make a difference in many people's experience with Chef. It's also validating to know that working hard can have a positive consequence.

I was with CX.com for almost a year when the company started having issues and was discussing a pivot. I took this opportunity to find a new job, and that took me a while. I worked for a short while at Scribd, and while I enjoyed my local coworkers, I struggled to work with our other systems administrator, who was based out of Canada.

I ended up moving to Simple.com almost two years ago, and it's been my happiest job experience since working in Boston. I'm able to learn and contribute, and my team is fantastic.

At this point in my life I'm very excited about where things are as well as upcoming challenges. I have a fantastic team at work and a fantastic girlfriend at home. I don't know what the future will hold, but I know that I will be able to overcome any challenges it may present. My love of computers, technology, and problem solving is still strong. I used to be afraid that not going to college and failing badly at school would limit my potential, but I know now that I am the only one who can define my potential.

TURN SIXTEEN AND START WITH NOTHING

4611 271719 5625538 375673 655702 825162
4713 674526 619522 862981 634717 897407

<COMMUNICATION ON THE JOB>

We've talked about how fast your interviewers and hiring managers evaluate you as a person. Now let's talk about how to make a great impression on your colleagues. These lessons will be helpful throughout your career. The tech workplace can be weird and tough to navigate, and there's a hard realization I (and other technologists I've talked to) have come to after making a chain of avoidable mistakes that led to getting fired: your skill set is not what gets you a job, nor is it what will determine your success at it. Your skill set is the requirement for getting in the door, and the rest of your career is based on how you treat people and how you allow yourself to be treated. These lessons are some of the hardest ones I've ever had to learn.

Somewhat ironically, we call people skills "soft skills." That is possibly the most misleading term I've ever seen. Part of the reason we call social skills "soft" is that a scientist cannot predict the right or wrong answer, and "soft" is actually something of an insult in the academic, technical, and scientific worlds. I'm a logical, strategic person, and acquiring "soft skills" has been the hardest task I've faced in my life. If you're a techie, chances are you have struggled at times with how to treat people, been frustrated with workplace politics, and been completely blindsided by a colleague's negative opinion of you.

People are forgiving of others who don't make the same mistakes again and again, and of people who use real compassion and integrity in their dealings with others. If you bring kindness and humility to your interactions with others, you'll find these situations a lot easier to handle, and your colleagues will have a better opinion of you than they would have otherwise. This isn't just going to be a list of things you should get done as you start out at a new job—it's about what kind of person you are and how you treat others.

DIFFERENT COMMUNICATION TOOLS FOR DIFFERENT SITUATIONS

Now we can get into the real details of the skills you should show to be a great developer and teammate. They all boil down to communication.

There are four major kinds of workplace communication. You're making first impressions constantly, and the way you communicate using digital, interpersonal, physical, and one-to-many communication tools will determine the course of your career.

Digital Communications

Instant messaging is a common tool in the tech workplace. Because so much tech work is now done in large rooms full of cubicles where quiet is needed and never supplied (because some wildly enthusiastic extrovert decided that developers needed to "cooperate" more and "synergize") and where no one can get the peace and solitude they need for doing hard brain work, it is impolite to shout across the room or get up, walk behind people, and tap some unsuspecting dev on the shoulder. Instead, use IM (instant messaging) as a knock on the door to ask quick yes-or-no questions and to get resources or links to learn on your own. For example, when you want to get a single piece of information, like a server address or a lunch time, ping someone on IM. "Pinging" means to send any kind of message that will notify the other person. It is generally used to refer to IM, due to the ping sound that an incoming message makes. It can also mean email. IM is less formal than email and is often used for friendly chats in an office, such as sending others jokes and links. Be aware of the office culture and whether or not sending jokes and links is appropriate. If coworkers have a busy status posted, IM them only if it is a real emergency for which you'd interrupt them in a private meeting. Server outages and fire drills are good examples.

Email is for more involved questions and status reports that may lead to a chain of communication. You can also use it to send a question to someone whose IM information you don't know yet or who is not signed into IM. Email discussion threads are important and often turn into documentation. Go easy on informal speech and emoticons until you know more about how people talk at your company. Spell out all words and, in general, treat email as if it were a document, not a text message. If you cannot write a decent email from your mobile device and you must do so for work, get a better digital or physical keyboard rather than using a "sent from my phone" sign-off line to excuse typos. Besides, it's no one's business but yours where you are and what device you're using. Email is important, it isn't going away soon, and you will be personally and professionally judged on how you write. Get rid of any cheery signature messages. If you have a sign-off line, it can be "Thanks" (a good default), "Respectfully" (very American military establishment), "Kind regards" (an excellent option to hide your cultural origins and the equivalent of a Transatlantic accent), or "Sincerely" (anachronistic but charming), and that is it. It's best to have a signature that contains your contact information and sign off using only your name. Do not use "Cheers" (how Americans think Brits close emails), as it is the single most irritating sign-off line in all of email history and annoys every human but you. Answer all your email at least once per day. The best rule you can possibly follow is to empty your inbox at least once per day; it's called the inbox zero rule, and I've been doing it for years. If you get behind on email, others will take it as a sign that you let details slide. Being responsible with your communication is hugely important for a job like development, and you need to be able to manage your instructions and documentation in order to code. Whatever your team uses to communicate should be treated with the same respect as an in-person conversation.

In-Person Communication

If you are shy or have communication issues, there is a great deal of help for you in your community. Join Toastmasters or attend a Dale Carnegie class. Your local community college will certainly have an introductory public speaking class—and you should take it. Volunteering at a local shelter or food bank can help you develop some healthy connections with others. Asking people you trust for their honest opinions about your professional communication style can also be helpful.

Notice that I didn't use the word "introvert" above when describing someone with communication problems. Introversion is not a problem or a deficit; it is a description of what activities drain a person's energy and what activities recharge that person's energy. Some of the world's greatest communicators and orators are introverts; this is because introverts take time away from people to think deeply about what they wish to say, practice their oratory, and assimilate information about how to improve with great efficiency. Abraham Lincoln, Mahatma Gandhi, and Barack Obama are all spectacular examples of classical and compelling orators, and they are all introverts. Software engineers and developers are also far more likely to be introverted. If someone on your team wants to be alone to think or needs peace and quiet to accomplish tasks, do not take it personally. It is not that you are a bad person or that they do not like you. It is only that your presence in the room and interacting with you is draining the energy your coworker needs to complete tasks. If any other person were in that room, it would be just as draining for your coworker.

Finally, if you are still having issues understanding how to interact with your team and have problems with communication, approach a private coach to get an evaluation of how your personality can be shown to best advantage. Sometimes we have an odd habit or a tic that can keep us from being able to best influence others, and simply knowing what it is can greatly improve our professional presence.

One of the things I work on is listening. I used to interrupt and cut people off all the time. I was doing it because I could already tell what they were going to say, already had a response for the next four things they'd say, and I was jumping the conversation forward for maximum efficiency while paying them what I thought was the compliment of assuming they could keep up. That's not how people interpret someone interrupting them, however, and I had to realize that the insult of cutting them off almost always cost me more time fixing the situation than just listening would have. I deliberately and with malice aforethought went and took a class on listening, which was just as touchy-feely and irritating to me as a technologist as you think it would be. I kept wanting to fix the way everyone spoke, and needed to realize that it was more important in interactions for the other person to feel heard than to minimize time spent in communication. It's much more efficient (long-term) to listen than to interrupt. You may also have a similar habit in communication, and if you approach it with compassion and an eye to the end goal, you'll be a better person and a better colleague.

Nonverbal Communication and Body Language

Humans are political animals who still operate on an unconscious level much as we did in the days of the cave, the meat, and the fire. The way we carry ourselves shows everyone around us at what rank in the tribe we expect to be placed and how we expect to be treated. We all have a lizard brain, an atavistic portion of our consciousness that tells us "Fire bad; tree pretty." It tells us when to run because a predator is near, when to strike to get the most meat, when to cower for fear of a Neanderthal more powerful than ourselves, and when to steal a weak kinsman's mate or food.

The way you walk, shake hands, stand, sit, and gesture sends millions of tiny messages to the lizard brains around you. Imagine a contrast between someone who stands up straight, walks with purpose, sits erect, and shakes hands firmly, as opposed to someone who leans, slinks, totters, sways, reclines, and extends a hand languidly. To which of these people would you grant authority, perhaps without even realizing it? Now the depressing bit—assign a gender to those two people. Which of those two archetypical kinds of body language belongs to a person who will be trusted with leadership? Which will be assigned to run a dev team or be elected to run a country? I did not specify a gender for either, but I imagine that you easily envisioned a male in the first role, perhaps John Wayne or John F. Kennedy, and in the second role, perhaps Paris Hilton or Sophia Loren.

Women are socially instilled with the body language of the latter stereotype, and women who use the first kind of body language can present a serious challenge of an unfamiliar kind to many men. Most people, not just men, are not used to the body language of authority and power coming from a woman, and it can cause a weird kind of cognitive disconnect to see it in action.

Try this exercise out. Tell a close male friend of yours (don't do this with your boss) you're going to try out some new body language. Push into his personal space, shake hands with him, and bare your teeth when you smile. Shake his hand harder than he is shaking yours. Get a smidge too close. Lean forward slightly as you do it. There's a reason this will feel creepy to you and weird to him; you are announcing with your body that you are more powerful than he is and that you are the apex predator in the relationship. This exercise should show you what happens when you go all the way over the top into a direct physical challenge with someone who's used to being the apex predator. Now let's use this principle of the lizard brain in a different way.

Here is how to use your understanding of body language. Stand up right now. Feel a string attached to the top of your skull, right in the center. Imagine that you are a marionette being suspended by that string. Stretch your entire spinal column upward. Move both your shoulders one full inch back. Imagine that your chin is resting on a table edge at a 90 degree angle. Twist the inner joint of both your elbows a half inch outward; you will feel the palms of your hands face more forward than inward. Stare at a point in front of you that is two feet higher than you normally focus your gaze. Slightly tense the transabdominal muscles just below your belly button; this will pull in your stomach slightly and lock your gut muscles to your spine. That is perfect posture. This posture will make you appear to be two inches taller than normal, especially if you slouch at all. Remember, height equals authority and increased salary. It's also good for your back and spine to stand up straight. Very petite women are sometimes unfortunately overlooked—literally. Taller people, including taller women, will have a difficult time yielding authority to someone over whose head they can easily see. If you are truly tiny, you can try using a slightly higher chair in your office than the chairs in front of your desk—and you can hide that you're doing it!

When you shake hands with someone, you must be firm. Young boys are encouraged to develop a firm handshake and are rewarded socially by doing so. Women who have been taught how to give a proper handshake find that it helps them every day in terms of authority and impressions. As a society, we use a handshake to indicate honor, trust, welcome, honesty, a bargain, goodwill, and manners. All these traits are associated with someone with whom you would very much like to work. In technology, we even use the technical term "handshake" to indicate that two computers have verified the others' identity and begun trusted communication.

To develop a good handshake, start with the basics of posture. Stand up straight as I have just taught you. Extend your right hand in a haymaker motion from your side; look down at your hand, and as you move it forward to shake hands with someone, do not stick it straight at them. Instead, draw an outward arc with your hand to give the other person the ability to use peripheral vision and depth perception in order to judge when and where to reach out. Pinch the webbing between your thumb and finger. That webbing on your hand should hit the webbing on the other person's hand first. Look at your hand, palm up. Leave your thumb sticking out, and curl your fingers into a fist. Do you see how the thumb naturally bends a bit inward when you do so? The thumb will hit the meat on the top of the other person's hand lightly; do not use pressure on the thumb. Instead, reach out, hit the webbing of the other person's hand, squeeze around the palm—not around the fingers, which crushes them together—pump twice to the beat from Soft Cell's "Tainted Love," smile, make eye contact, and greet the person. Go watch the Ignite talk I did on giving a good handshake. You can also practice by shaking hands with everyone you meet with, whether you know them or not. They'll either be happy for the contact or they'll dismiss your oddity as you practice.

A note for left-handed people: sorry. In the USA, you must shake with your right hand. It is not personal; it is a rule just as driving on the right or left side of the road is a rule depending on where you are in the world. Forms of greeting may be different elsewhere in the world, involving a kiss, a bow, or a spoken phrase, but in the United States, you have to have a good old-fashioned all-American handshake to seal deals and to introduce yourself to be seriously considered for any people-facing job.

On hugs: learn to do the professional hug. This may sound extremely strange, but believe it or not, technologists (especially on the West Coast) are actually very "huggy." My theory is that it's because we're mostly alone all day long and at least subconsciously seeking human contact. If you're extremely against that kind of physical touch, then opt out for everyone. If you do hug people, practice the one-armed hug that's halfway between a handshake and a full-body embrace where you grasp the other person's hand, pull them in for a left-handed quick backslap or squeeze, and then release them. It's closely related to the "bro-hug." Hugging is an actual professional skill, and among younger people is starting to replace the handshake altogether. You should definitely learn to hug in such a way that people are not uncomfortable with you. While there are a million variations on the hug, this version that's a half handshake and half embrace is the best compromise I've found between seeming unfriendly and plastering my body all over some business development professional who's three scotches deep already and likely to get handsy.

Public Speaking and Presentations

Speaking to people is not the same thing as talking with people. Knowing how to speak to others is the key skill for promotion, leadership, management, and getting your way. Talking to people is a two-way street. You're learning how to create a bond and figuring out what the other person wants and needs, and there is a presumption that you are on an equal level. Speaking to people is fundamentally unequal. You are beginning with the proposition that you need to tell people something they do not already know or persuade them to think or act differently than they already do, and you are focused on transferring communication from you to them. Often, we do not even follow those verbs with the same directional prepositions. We speak to people, and we talk with people. Women are often extremely uncomfortable with the idea of speaking in public.

It's time to get over it. Taking over a room with the strength of your personality, forcing people to listen to you, and convincing them to change their behavior is a powerful series of actions, and you must learn to be an effective leader. Eventually, you will need to speak up in a meeting, make a presentation or share a spoken report with a senior team, lead a group, and get promoted. You are going to take the technical world by storm, and you can't do that if you let others take advantage of the fact that you are nervous about speaking in public.

If there is any single skill that you can learn that will convince others in their guts that you have leadership potential, it is the art of persuasive public speaking. Note that I do not just say public speaking here. Persuasive public speaking is quite different than simply standing in front of your boss and your boss's boss and reading a report aloud. Though I said earlier that speaking to people primarily involves the transfer of information from you to them, there is information flowing from your audience to you as well. Something to remember: persuasive speaking is not something that you were born knowing how to do. No one knows how to speak persuasively automatically or how to sway people to their side without practice. Even Bill Clinton, certainly the most convincing, charismatic, persuasive public speaker since Dr. Martin Luther King Jr., had to learn to form his arguments, listen to his audience with his eyes, and alter his tone and form to match what he was constantly estimating was the best possible outcome for his speech. This is a skill that you will be learning and practicing your entire life. There is a very good reason why politicians always sound so smooth and convincing—they practice for hours every single day.

There are thousands of books out there on how to improve your public speaking. However, you can get most of the benefit of systematically learning public speaking by remembering to build a simple argument with three persuasive points.

- Introduction: "Here is a problem that I want to solve with you here today."
- Thesis: "Here's what you need to do to help me solve it."
- Point 1 (Reasonable): Supporting reason one with a sentence stating the gist of the evidence and some supporting facts that show that common sense, scientific evidence, and members of their community are on your side.
- Point 2 (Positive): Supporting reason two with a sentence stating the gist of the evidence and some supporting facts that show that if they help you solve this problem, the world will be a better place, they will make more money, they will be promoted, or some other good thing will happen.
- Point 3 (Negative): Supporting reason three with a sentence stating the gist of the evidence and some supporting facts that show that if they don't help you solve this problem, something dreadful will happen: they will lose money, their children will fail in school, or the apocalypse will descend.
- Conclusion: "For those three reasons with their supporting facts, you should give my cause money, change how you feel about this political issue, invest in my company, give me flex time and let me telecommute, or do whatever else I am asking. Now, can I sign you up, put you in touch with my CFO, or add that to my calendar?"

Basically, state the problem, give them reasons to believe you and support you, and make the ask at the end. Learn to actually ask for what you want. Do not assume that this is obvious to your audience. If you learned to write a five-paragraph essay in school, this format will sound quite familiar to you. After two decades of work that has always involved persuading people to do what I need them to do, I have found that this is the easiest format to practice and alter while using, and the easiest way to get the job done.

The best way to get started is to volunteer to speak on behalf of a cause in which you believe. Do you support blood drives? Find out at your local Red Cross if you can volunteer to do workplace presentations. You'll take some materials to a local workplace and do a five-minute speech to get the employees signed up to donate blood. Do you believe in children's literacy? (I suppose a better question is, who doesn't?) Volunteer at your local library to read to children at a preset time each week. The key is to do something that is meaningful to you. Your own passion for the subject will help you as you persuade people to be better, help more, and work for the benefit of others.

Listen with your eyes. Your audience is not using their words; you must be able to interpret body language. When people lean back in their chairs, shuffle, fail to look you in the eye, and sigh, that's a sign that what you are doing isn't working. Don't worry about fixing it during the speech itself unless you're very witty; humor is the universal solution to a bored audience. Fix it afterward by asking someone to tell you honestly how you could have improved.

Finally, you're a real public speaker when you can change minds with your words. Talk people into giving blood if they're afraid, talk a parent into volunteering at the local junior high, or talk someone into not parking in the disability spot at the grocery store "just for a minute." When you've done that, you can handle any board room in the world.

<THE FAMILY>

I don't much like the phrase "mommy wars." It implies that the life-ending, wildly expensive, soul-sucking, career-ending, hugely burdensome problem of bringing forth the next generation of humanity rests solely on the beleaguered shoulders of women. Men are starting to be part of the discussion. Still, until we have national policies in place that offer real, reasonable ways to combine a career and the spawning forthwith of that next generation, let's take a moment to figure out what having children and a family in tech actually means.

THE REAL PROBLEM

I am a stepmom, but I never had a baby while in office, so to speak. I'm more familiar with the opposite experience: workers coming to me and telling me that they're going to become parents. I can tell you now that the biggest problem managers and bosses face is not the fact that tech workers have children, but the fact that every one of them deeply, deeply underestimates (1) the amount of time a child will take and (2) the amount of time needed to spin back up from parental leave.

I want you to notice something. Even though I never used a gendered pronoun or specified that it was women tech workers asking me for leave, you likely assumed it was, in fact, women getting pregnant.

Actually, it's mostly men now telling me that they're going to become parents. Inevitably, they do the same exact thing that women used to do, which is assure me thoroughly that they have a plan and that they know how much time they need away.

They don't.

I'm blown away by the fact that tech engineers, who perfectly sensibly multiply all tech product and feature delivery dates by π, as $DEITY and all humanity intended, fail to do the same thing with their own human product delivery. Even though our culture fails to offer any sort of meaningful universal parental leave, stop thinking that you can be back at work a week after you have become a parent. It's not realistic, and you'll be exhausted and likely resentful that you can't be there for your child. Don't put the people you work with in the terrible position of telling you that it's not that they hate parents, it's that you are causing more work for everyone and should have taken more recovery time.

Having children is going to change your life, and you and your workplace have a lot of (often very screwed-up) expectations about how that change will manifest. Let's look at your expectations and the expectations of your workplace, and see if we can find some overlapping ground on which we can build you a comeback plan.

EXPECTATIONS

It is totally unrealistic for parents to take years away from their careers to have children and expect to be automatically leveled-up to the place their colleagues are at. You also cannot expect that if you are the single full-stack web developer at a six-person startup, you can take a year off and come back to the same position you left. Children will interrupt your career plans. If you want to have them, go for it, but understand that doing so will incur a penalty on your career timeline. You are choosing to spend time with your children instead of your career, and it really is not possible to have it all. Fortunately, childcare seems to be trending toward a more equitable split.

I'm totally OK with saying the above, because as a tech manager, like I said, it's actually more men now coming to me and requesting parental leave. I've never had a conversation with a male engineer in which he told me that he'd have to take off three months and also expected to stay a project lead all the way through and come back with a promotion.

Also, let's be totally honest: if you take a year off, that is a year of experience and skills you won't have. Personally, I would be furious to find out that someone who'd left a career to have children and had less work experience and skills than I do was promoted over my head. Affirmative action and equal opportunity was never and is not intended to let people with fewer skills and less experience triumph over those with more. It was intended to aid a decision between two people who have the same set of skills. If one of them had to overcome more obstacles to get to that point of equal skills, I'm already inclined to give that person some extra credit . . . but I'm never going to give a job to someone who can't do it over someone who can.

So what's the real thing you need to know? Children will interrupt your life. It's OK that they'll do so. They'll also interrupt your job. However, that doesn't mean that your career stops in its place—only that you need a good plan for parallel action. Begin thinking of yourself as needing a comeback plan. You're going to plan in advance for how to come back with new killer skills parallel to the work you would have done but which are not a substitute for it.

Early-Stage Startups versus Established Tech Companies

Early-stage startups are not for you if you want to take substantial time off from your job to become a parent and expect to come back to the same role you left. I have never seen a primary caregiver parent with no nanny successfully found and exit a startup or do well in the first through tenth hired roles as a new parent, though I do personally know of one woman who had a lot of support and managed to sell her early-stage tech startup. This is because early-stage startups are not covered by parental leave laws. According to Business Management Daily, "the Pregnancy Discrimination Act (PDA) prohibits discrimination against employees and applicants on the basis of 'pregnancy, childbirth and related medical conditions.' Any employer that's subject to Title VII of the Civil Rights Act of 1964 (i.e., has 15 or more employees) must comply with the PDA." So until you are a company of at least fifteen people (and after the lion's share of the equity and top positions have been assigned), you have no rights in terms of pregnancy discrimination. The level of logistics to handle administrative HR for maternity leave hasn't even been considered yet when there are only three engineers, a technical marketer, and a CEO. If you take six months of leave from that company, it will either shut down or you will be removed from the equity stock pile and replaced.

I think the real conflict here comes from two uncomfortable truths. At an established tech company, if you take leave, there is enough logistical support in your company and enough people in duplicate roles as yours that your absence will be inconvenient but not company threatening, and while you may be important to the company, the building won't collapse if you're not there. At an early-stage startup, you are vital to the existence of the company and have a lot of power and unique abilities, in which case leaving the company for an extended period of time necessitates your immediate replacement or can severely damage the company.

Here's the truly rotten corollary to those two truths: women don't generally get promoted to those vital roles unless they create them themselves or do not have children. I have, in fact, seen women CEOs with children, because they started the company themselves after their children were in school, or because they built in their own ability to create leave for themselves in the future when they decided to take some time to have children. They are also not usually the primary caregiver (or they have really good childcare). Marissa Mayer, the CEO of Yahoo, is not the primary caregiver for her small children; she has nannies on staff and administrators to handle her personal life so that she can enjoy the time she has with her children. Good for her; she's living her life as she sees fit. But don't pretend that if you can't hire a nanny and a personal assistant and you are the primary caregiver for small children that you can have Marissa Mayer's life and be in an early-stage startup.

Here's yet another icky corollary: the reason there are zero female tech billionaires (Meg Whitman, CEO of Hewlett-Packard, is the only female billionaire connected to tech that I know of, and she is an executive and politician, not a technologist or programmer) is that only early-stage startup founders have the kind of equity that means they can hit the jackpot if their company succeeds (after having made the sacrifice of time and life it takes to get the company up), and in our current environment, women are not supported by venture capital and angel investors if they have the barest whiff of mommy about them. I'm not going to talk about the depressing numbers around women founders and venture capital right here. That's a whole other book. Instead, I'll give you some good ideas on how to create ongoing career options for yourself that let you get good parental leave and still have a great résumé.

THE COMEBACK PLAN

Here's what you'll want to do with your parental leave. First and foremost, take off enough time. Multiply your timeline estimate by π at every point. I don't want to see a new parent (male or female) back at work for a bare minimum of six weeks, and if you take six months, good for you.

Second, have a real conversation with your manager about whether you will need to be replaced and what your options are for coming back with the same status. If you think they're not telling you the truth, go over their head. It's common in tech for maternity leave policies to be lagging behind those in other industries because of the dearth of women—the situation just hasn't come up before and may not until their hundredth or two hundredth employee. Be prepared with a sample maternity leave policy that you can hand to them and offer as an option. Get promises in writing and lay out a leave and return schedule on paper with your manager's sign-off. It doesn't matter how many times you were told that your company wouldn't penalize you for having a baby. If you don't have a clear plan down on paper, it will be very easy for a manager or supervisor to claim that in the grip of hormones, you just missed something. If you cannot negotiate leave or if you think that your leave request is going to be a problem, consult an employment attorney. Paying $500 for a consult now will seem real damn cheap if you come back to a demotion later. Most companies will not consciously take advantage of you, but just the act of laying out your return plan on paper will make your manager and supervisor envision your return and deliberately plan for it. Consider approaching a maternity leave consultant or referring your company to one if no one has ever taken maternity leave from your company—or even if someone has.

Third, remember that even if you're right about the date you will come back to work, many timelines can get messy with children around. Work hard to be that same responsible human when you show back up in the office. I've heard that hiring a virtual assistant for a few months can be extremely helpful. Good virtual assistants can be booked very inexpensively on a part-time, weekly basis to do nothing but call you and remind you to do things and help you adhere to deadlines. The second-biggest source of collegial annoyance besides taking up the slack for a missing colleague is a lack of reliability when that colleague returns. Try to undercommit for a few months. It's better to be extremely reliable at 75 percent capacity than scattered at 100 percent capacity.

Fourth, start your own company as covered in the Start Your Own Company chapter. This is especially relevant if you're intending to be the primary caregiver. It will be a simple way for you to maintain an employment record as an open source software developer and technical consultant. You're doing this so that your résumé has no gaps. You're going to do at least a little development while you're out of the office, and it might as well be under your own shingle. Many more instructions are included in that chapter, including strategies on clients and branding. I've also seen a lot of primary caregivers successfully transition from being FTE employees at larger tech companies to being freelancers after they have children. They tended to plan it carefully by building their consultancies while they were fully employed so that after they had children, they could come back at a slower pace and start handling flexible freelance careers. You'll use the exact same instructions in starting your own company, but you'll actually be working to build it into a lifestyle business for yourself instead of using it as a cover for your résumé gaps.

Fifth, enjoy becoming a parent! There's a lot of guilt and frustration around children and careers. Unfortunately, for the foreseeable future in tech, it'll continue to be hard to balance your job and your children. I hope that you take at least a little extra time for yourself, just because you need it, and that you really enjoy it. If you have started your own consulting company to cover résumé gaps, a week or so won't matter to the outside world, but it will matter to you and your new child. I'm glad that more smart, open-minded, talented people feel able to become new parents, and I hope you enjoy this part of your life.

NEGOTIATING YOUR FAMILY COMMITMENTS

Who's the Primary Caregiver?

This is honestly more of an issue with heterosexual couples who have assortatively mated. That is social science jargon for two people who have gotten married and have equally successful and fulfilling careers. But the minute the woman gets pregnant, the unspoken assumption is that she's lost any chance of ever really making it in her career again.

Once I was talking with a male friend of mine who was dating someone and considering a longer commitment. I asked him if, when they had children, he'd be the one staying home so her career could get back on track. He looked at me with total incomprehension—not because he was a bad person but because no one had ever told him that he might be the one making the sacrifices in the relationship so his partner (who, by the way, was likely to have a more lucrative career) could make the alpha paycheck. This is one of those places where unconscious social bias creeps in and where the dog that doesn't bark will bite you later.

Have a very serious conversation with your partner about who will be the primary caregiver. There are lots of options for you, including the 50/50 model of parenting. I cannot tell you what will work for you, but I can tell you that if you don't talk in advance about who is simply expected to know which brand of cough syrup to buy and whose job it is to handle midnight feedings, it's very easy to slip into traditional gender roles without thinking. Don't not think.

The Second Shift

This section is going to be deeply personal, and I actually asked for my husband's permission to talk about it. I know how horrible that sounds, but trust me—to get this personal, you'd want to check with your spouse too.

My husband, Dean, and I have had to negotiate so many things in our marriage. One of the biggest things is the housework. The only reason I was able to write this book is that he and I added a housekeeper line item into our budget. This line item got added a few years ago after I exploded like a screaming shrew at him for not taking the garbage out because all he had to do was take out the trash, which takes him like five minutes, and I've spent two hours scrubbing the bathrooms because he can't manage to get his shavies in the sink, and I can't DO ten hours at a coding job and come home to four hours of cooking and cleaning and *I love you but I'm going to murder you in your sleep.*

We left the house to have the rest of the conversation about what a Second Shift is and why I can't do it.

There is a demon in the back of my head that tells me I cannot work in my house if it's not clean and that if anyone comes over to see my house, it's my fault that it's not spotless. I was raised by a stay-at-home mom who was, among other terrifying things, a drill instructor in the army. I know, without any shadow of a doubt, that if someone does, in fact, come over to our house, it will be my fault that the house is not clean. There is approaching-zero social expectation that if the place isn't clean, Dean should be the one doing something about it.

I am not alone.

The job of homemaking falls to women in utterly ridiculous proportions compared to men. Dean thinks that by buying a sandwich at the grocery store, he's saving me cleanup time in the kitchen. He's not. He thinks that a picked-up house is a clean house. It is not.

You can sense a little of my crazy peeking through here, right?

I was built this way by a society and a family and a religion that told me constantly in my formative years that it's the woman's fault if the home isn't warm, clean, welcoming, and gently scented of freshly baked chocolate chip cookies. I don't know how to fix that training in my head, and Dean doesn't know how to fix it, either. It's also not his job to fix it. It's more my place to forgive myself if the house isn't perfect.

See the language I used there without even thinking? I have to "forgive" myself for not having a clean house, because it's my problem and my job to fix it as fast as I can! What a double-load of horsefeathers.

I'm really hoping that you don't have the same programming as I do. If you do, I'm hoping that we're the last generation that does have this programming. I'll have that demon in the back of my head as long as I live, and I satiate him with a housekeeper for three hours every two weeks. It's OK to buy liberty and utility with money instead of physical possessions. Acknowledging this fact can save your career and relationships.

The best thing I can tell you about how to handle your Second Shift, especially if you have some of the same generational issues I do, is to negotiate with your partner before you enter into a life-long agreement. Dean and I negotiated much, much more than most people do, and even we didn't cover everything that was going to happen. Try keeping a log of the time you spend on housework; there are apps for that now. Do a real, honest accounting of the time you're spending cooking and cleaning, and be real with your partner not just about the time but about why you have to spend it. One lovely result of our society becoming more acceptant of nontraditional family structures is that in gay couples, this kind of negotiating has to happen in a mindful way, which is providing a great example for heterosexual couples to emulate.

Last but not least, don't brain your spouse with a mop handle when they say "Have you considered just not cleaning the house so often?" Blood is very sticky, and you'll just have to redo the floors.

The Truth

Tech is one of the harder careers to succeed at if you're a primary caregiver for children or family members. Unfortunately, until free, quality childcare is a right and not a privilege, a successful tech career is still very difficult for parents to attain. I want to give you the best possible chance to succeed, but the outlook is frankly bleak when it comes to being a primary caregiver having a baby in tech—and this applies to men and women both. I cudgeled my brain for great, positive, helpful examples of women who have succeeded in tech as primary caregivers, and the truth is that I know only one—her name is Katie Cunningham, and lucky for you, she wrote a chapter in this book. To be fair, many women keep the fact that they're primary caregivers quiet and off social media for fear of harming their careers, so I might know more who simply aren't as open as Katie has been about it. I know many women who have succeeded in tech with children, but they either had enough money in advance that they could pay for primary caregiving (a nanny or daycare) or they had a stay-at-home spouse.

You do have the option to detour into gigs, writing, speaking, teaching, and paratechnical jobs like digital marketing or project management. It's part of the reason you often find women in technical marketing jobs and middle management in tech; those positions tend to be more interchangeable, flexible, and able to accommodate caregiving. By their nature they're jobs created later on in tech companies, and there tend to be multiple such positions in any company, meaning that if you come back from parental leave, you can likely come back at the same pay rate and level, even if you're not with the same team. Be careful, though, and make that decision thoughtfully; it's very easy to move from a technical to a nontechnical position, but it's very difficult to go the other direction.

I hope that with all the innovation in our world, we'll soon see more flexibility and changing expectations in technology when it comes to parenting options.

Throughout this book, I've had to carefully balance being optimistic and being honest. I believe the best way to keep women in tech is to relay the collective experiences of women so that you don't feel isolated when you start to see these issues. We can all work together to changed the experiences of women in this industry if, and only if, we know we're not alone.

THE EDUCATOR
Kristin Toth Smith

I was a musician, an actor, and a singer. I was a writer. I was a dancer. I was a runner. I was a daddy's (and grandpa's) girl. And I happened to be good at math. I believe most of my mom's thirties were spent driving me from one thing to another while I explored every possible activity that I might love or thrive doing.

And it worked. When things really got serious (or so it seemed—I just needed to figure out what I was going to do after high school), I was staring down a most diverse set of options.

I wanted to go to the University of Southern California and be a music major. (My summer orchestra director was the dean of music there.)

I wanted to go to Notre Dame. (I cringe while I write this because of where I ended up.) If I had gone there, I would have been prelaw.

I wanted to go to New York University . . . well, because it was in New York City, and I had never been there, but it sounded AWESOME.

I wanted to go to Northwestern and become a journalist. (This seemed to be an epidemic among my friends, probably because the First Gulf War broke out while we were in our formative career years.)

And I figured, well, even though it's in state, the University of Michigan is a pretty good school for a lot of things. (Ha! I didn't really appreciate the school only fifty miles away from home.) My reasoning: "*If* I apply, I should probably apply to the College of Engineering because it's easier to transfer out than to transfer in later." Plus my dad had been an engineer and my grandfather had been an engineer, and I thought they had had pretty great lives.

When it was time to choose, Michigan had not only the benefits of close-by free laundry and a home-cooked meal on occasion but also a scholarship and in-state tuition. (My parents made it very clear that they would somehow figure out how to send me anywhere I wanted to go, but the burden that would have put on my family seemed pretty big at the time.) So I went off to engineering school. (They had the coolest toys on the engineering campus too!)

As luck would have it, I had gone to a high school with a pretty great academic record, and my first semester was really strong. At that same time, the business and engineering schools were cooking up a program that partnered the two in the pursuit of building a new generation of manufacturing talent. While I wasn't incredibly interested in manufacturing, the study sounded really appealing—business, foreign language, engineering, and a master's degree while you're at it—and it seemed like a pretty responsible way to choose not-choosing. Plus there was another scholarship involved. So I became locked into engineering—in fact, two engineering degrees.

I found that I really liked it (not thermo, but a lot of the other classes) after a while. It was a lot of problem solving and thinking with different perspectives to break the rules, build new things, and make services, processes, or products better.

I did a project about e-commerce just before graduation. It was not only an interesting topic—how do you use this new, crazy thing called the Internet to connect with your customers in new ways—but also included three months in Boulder, Colorado, for the summer. The introduction of technology into the equation completed my sphere of interests. When I graduated a few months later, I left for Austin, Texas, to work at Dell. I would be manufacturing computers in new ways and working for one of the biggest e-commerce brands around.

It was so much fun. I got to work on really tough problems. How can we build a manufacturing facility with less than two hours of raw materials inventory? How can we mass customize every product but achieve benchmark mass production efficiencies? I had no idea, really. And then—because I had liked the ideas around e-commerce in my project in Colorado—someone thought, "Kristin likes technology and understands manufacturing operations. She can lead the software and hardware redesign for this new manufacturing facility." All I can say about this thought process was that they must have been desperate. I knew how to run decently interesting mathematical models in Excel or using stochastic modeling software, but I didn't have the first clue what the difference between a router and switch was or how you developed software (outside of my experience in a few computer science classes—Fortran, Pascal, Visual Basic). But I said, as I have so many times since, "Let's figure this out."

So I went back to my known skills. I walked the manufacturing line. I looked at what was happening. I looked at where they were scanning a barcode or plugging in a computer. I looked at the screens that were in front of the technicians. I found out why the lights came on in certain places. I started mapping it out. Since I could understand what I was seeing from the industrial engineering perspective, I started drawing boxes, asking questions, and filling in the blanks. I figured out that we were using eight major software systems. I talked to the managers of each team and asked if the engineer who knew the most about that team's software system could come to a meeting with the other manufacturing system engineers. And then I invited a networking engineer, a server and data center engineer, and the project manager for the data center in our building to a meeting.

That meeting came, and oh my, I was so nervous. I thought, *Here I am, a clueless twenty-three-year-old pulling together all these super technical guys*—yes, they were all men—*and I'm going to present this guess of a process map with all of these question marks and blanks in it.* All I could hope was that they would be kind and help me fill in the chart.

I was shocked. Not only were they kind, but they kept saying how helpful it was to see what the other software was doing, how their software worked with other systems, and even how it was used. It was a genuinely lively discussion in which everyone had more questions than I did, and for the most part we could, as a team, answer the most important ones. This became a weekly meeting for the duration of the project, and although I had every manufacturing leader tell me that these "IT guys" were never going to deliver on the promises they made me, we delivered thirty-two software changes to these eight systems, on time. We were the only part of the new manufacturing plant project that was ready on our launch date! And the changes *WORKED . . . LIKE WE WANTED THEM TO.* All those naysayers said nothing. I didn't really care. It was so fulfilling to see how much we accomplished and the team was so cohesive and happy that it didn't matter. We cele-brated. We laughed. We knew what we had accomplished.

During this project, the team who was working on the stuff I *should* have been working on (if we were going by my degrees) was filled with the most brilliant, down-to-earth, and fun col-leagues. We bonded in a truly special way that I now recognize happens when you work on a high-stakes, risky, time-intensive project together, especially when you feel as if you have little support from anyone else. You become family in so many ways. Many of them had done a program through MIT that was oriented toward manufacturing and operations, similar to the one I did at Michigan. I had once (while at UM) thought that it would be fun to be the only person to go through both programs. (I'm naturally competitive like this.) Now that I knew what kind of people were in the program, I started thinking about it even more.

Eventually, the dot-com boom slowed, and most of the fun proj-ects I was working on after we opened the manufacturing plant were decommissioned. We stopped making investments in supply chain software companies and put XML standards on hold (both my projects). I started getting anxious for more challenges. I kept thinking about my friends from that MIT program and the goal I had given myself to be the only one to do both the Michigan and MIT programs. Since it seemed like a challenge and a little scary, I said, "Why not?"

I applied. I took the GMAT. (I bought study guides for both the GMAT and the LSAT, but every lawyer I talked to told me not to go into law. I took it as sound advice and focused on business school.) I thought about applying for other schools and other programs, but I figured, *If I get into this program at MIT, I'll decide whether I want to go or not. If I don't, I will see if I still want to go to school next year.* If this seems flippant, I really don't mean it that way. A huge reason I could even consider attending the program was that, if I got in, it came with a full-ride scholarship. A couple of months later, Don, one of the initial founders and the then-director of the program, called me on a Saturday morning while I was making pancakes. I was accepted! Holy $H!*!!! (By the way, each one of us accepted into this program remembers exactly where we were when we got the phone call from Don.)

Deciding whether to go to MIT once I was accepted was much more difficult than (a) most would think and (b) it should have been. I did spreadsheet models of the payoff versus opportunity cost. I made lists of pros and cons. I talked to everyone I knew (not everyone said to go, by the way). Then I had lunch with a guy I knew but not well. He told me this: "Look, I bet you have lists and models and a host of assumptions and scenarios. You will drive yourself crazy trying to quantify what the outcome of going to school will be. Instead, think of this: What do you want to do for the next two years? Do you want to get more experience or go learn?" That was it. The idea of moving to a new place, meeting some new people, and spending every day investing in myself and learning something was definitely what I wanted. If I could do that at a place where I was likely to be the stupidest person in the room every day, even better. It sounded really challenging and sort of scary, so I said, "Let's do it."

Here's a quick little story that I need to share. When we were accepted to this program, we were each invited to a weekend on campus to meet the other prospective students, professors, and current students. It was beautiful. (I had previously believed that the crews rowing on the Charles River during the sunset scene was something that was staged for TV shows—it's not, by the way. It's truly there, every single evening.) But what was super striking was the first part of the weekend, when we all gathered and sat in a semicircular classroom with no one knowing another soul. One by one, we went around the room and introduced ourselves. Nearly to a one, these brilliant and accomplished people, sitting in a classroom at MIT after having been admitted to a highly selective program there, each confessed to probably being "the one who slipped by the admissions office." Yeah, impostor syndrome is everywhere.

I'm going to skip talking about MIT too much. It truly was a great experience, and I learned so much more than I could have ever expected and met some incredible people. I'm going to skip ahead to a time in 2002 when an executive from Amazon came and talked to our class.

I know him pretty well now, and I really can't think of a better role model in so many ways, but at the time, he seemed unreal: optimistic, wickedly smart, and fun, and working for a company actually looking to ask "why not" and never rest. Not only did he represent the company well, but the company was truly thinking about everything differently than any other company I had ever heard about. They had just launched free super-saver shipping; given today's e-commerce environment, it is hard to accurately describe how big this was at the time. It seemed like financial suicide. And they had started leveraging their operations infrastructure as a product and sharing what they had learned to do with others. They were trying to solve the problems that most companies thought of as given constraints or unsolvable or just physical laws. It just sounded so challenging. I wasn't really sure if I would measure up, but I decided I wanted to try to work for them.

When I interviewed at Amazon, it was challenging in the best possible way. I had really fun, intellectual conversations about complex and ambiguous opportunities that I had never thought through before. I realized that at Amazon I was pretty likely to work with smart, motivated people from whom I would learn a ton. I got a job offer. Actually, I got three. And after graduation, I packed up and moved out to Seattle knowing no one and feeling as scared and overwhelmed as I had in nearly every transition I had made up to that point. But again, since this seemed as if it would be challenging and a little scary, I said, "Let's do it."

Amazon was a PhD program in stretching, learning, and taking on a ton of responsibility without ever feeling as if it was happening. Sure, you knew you were working hard and working on tough challenges. But you were surrounded by others doing the same thing, and every time something interesting, challenging, and a little (or very) scary came around, I volunteered. I wanted to build things. I wanted to find ways to use a bunch of existing tools and processes in new ways, with some important modifications, to build experiences and products previously thought impossible. And I got to.

The recurring theme at Amazon (and then ever since) was the way that understanding the business, the operations, or the data *and* thinking about the design and architecture of where software could create a world-class experience, optimize a process, or create insight into the most important inner-workings of a system, process, or offering was truly the secret sauce of moving from something working to something exceptional. The fact that I had a business background and a deep understanding of operations but also understood technology—how it is built, how the people who code think, the way that different systems need to work together, what technology could solve and what humans did better—was a special skill. Most people could not straddle these two areas, and most of the opportunities lay in this crossover of both sides of the company—tech and business.

Eight years went by in a flash. I built some seriously fun stuff while I was there, and I met some of the most incredible people. But most of all, I learned a ton—not the least of which was just how much (quality, not quantity) I could do. When a startup across town called because they were building everything from scratch, I wondered if I truly would be able to build something without the infrastructure and support of all of these great people, systems, and security. It sounded extremely challenging and a little bit scary, so I said, "Let's do it!"

A few years later, I was reflecting on the fact that I had always been surrounded and enabled by software and that so many people who were not on the dev team were so intimidated or clueless about software. And yet software was really what was powering, improving, and making possible everything I had worked on for my entire career. It was also what was limiting how fast or how much we could progress and build the business. No matter what, we couldn't hire even a small fraction of the software developers that we really needed to build the business, improve customer experience, and improve the working lives of our employees. Periodically, we'd go through our goals for the business and prioritize them. We'd then allow the software team leaders to take a look at the high-level scope for the pieces of these goals that were dependent upon technology projects, estimate the time needed to run these projects, look at current staffing, estimate the software developers who would be hired away from us and the number we could hire, and then draw a line beneath their best estimate of which projects they could feasibly accomplish in that next period. That line was always, always, always very near to the top of a very long list of incredibly important projects.

After momentarily thinking I should go back to school and pursue computer science, my brain kicked into problem-solving and brainstorming mode. This problem wasn't new—and it was getting worse instead of better. There were so many things that seemed

to suggest that there is a real solution to this constant and growing problem that was keeping companies, large and small, from
realizing their potential. At the time, I was also thinking about the
fact that there were so many students graduating from universities
with huge student debt who were struggling to find jobs.

I reflected on the fact that technology was so rapidly evolving
that even those with degrees in CS were constantly buying books
about new languages and teaching themselves the things they
were using every day. It wasn't as if you could be an eternal expert
professional software developer without some work. And software
was something you could learn from a book or online courses.
And even more importantly, you could judge software developers by the quality of their code versus their degrees or which
schools they attended. It truly was a profession where many of the
most famous and accomplished professionals didn't have college
degrees. So if there were so many people who were unemployed
or underemployed, and they could learn to code, couldn't we
solve this big problem of not having enough software developers
to do what I wanted to with education?

This seemed like a very strange thing for me to say at the time.
I had a stint in high school when I was a teacher—violin lessons—
and I was pretty sure that I wasn't really cut out to be in education.
But I could think back to all of the opportunities that formal—and
experiential—education had given me, how much I had managed
to learn, and where it had taken me in my life. I remembered how
transformative education could be. And I wanted to do something
about it. I had been inching toward more formal involvement in
institutions of higher education—volunteering, organizing, and
advising. I figured I might one day teach a class or two. But this
idea about something that looked a little different and that I might
be able to impact today was—OK, by now you get it—challenging
and a little bit scary. So guess what. I said, "Let's do it!"

The first idea I had was a shared concept with a friend to create a nonprofit that would take entrepreneurship and technology
as enabling concepts into high schools in the parts of town that

were less wealthy and where students had fewer obvious options in front of them. I still think this is a fantastic idea—but I'm not the one to run a nonprofit. I'm just not cut out for it.

In the process of exploring and developing this idea, though, I had met the founder of Code Fellows, a vocationally oriented intensive training program for software developers. They were looking for some help as they started to scale, and even though I had started advising and consulting with a couple of startups, I made time to help out when I could. I was struck by the fact that it was working, this concept of education in technology as a transformative force for the individual and the collective idea of creating talent pipelines for companies that so sorely needed them.

We could make immediate impact. People were learning and finding their superpowers in software development. They could build things from nothing. More importantly, it was a springboard for them to find incredibly rewarding, lucrative, and in-demand jobs. And most importantly, it allowed them to improve their lives. And companies were able not only to fill open jobs but to start to build pipelines around a faster cadence of graduates who had practical, relevant skills and could hit the ground running . . . and could learn anything they needed to learn quickly.

It's not easy. The work is never done. But to see the effect that this education can have on a host of big challenges is incredibly rewarding both professionally and personally. It's also challenging for me, because I can't teach the technical skills, so leading a team has been another big risk for me. However, as I've gotten to the core of this challenge and become a part of the solution, it's become clear that continuing to help education evolve and work for students and the world at large will be part of my life from here on out. Let's do it!

<PERSONAL BRANDING>

There is only one thing in life worse than being talked about,
and that is not being talked about.
—OSCAR WILDE

This is the high-class problem chapter—also known as "I have a job, so how do I turn it into a career?" Personal branding is definitely atop the hierarchy of human needs. If you're worried about feeding yourself and paying the bills, it's fine to focus on getting the job first before grappling with how you're being seen on social media. If you have student loans and you have a job offer with a very staid and buttoned-up company that disapproves of gamers or goths or potheads or women with body hair, just take it. Feed and house yourself first, then worry about your image and whether you're in the right job. That being said, this is a serious issue during your mid-career, when you have some career stability and are now working on your long-term goals. If you've found yourself in a dead-end job with no promotion in sight, it's time to change your perspective. It's no longer just about your skill set; it's about your network, your image, and your personal brand.

I'm going to talk about three things in this chapter: being genuine, being findable, and being bold. At the end of this chapter, you'll know why it's better to have some people not like you than to have no one know you.

BE GENUINE

Don't Hide Who You Are

In the brave new world of the Internet, there's no way to hide who and what you are any longer. I have a lot of different identities. I'm an entrepreneur, a poker player, a CEO, a comic book aficionado, a hacker, a wife, a college professor, a triathlete, a cosplayer, an actor, a musician, a gamer, and much, much more. Some of these identities are (or seem to be) mutually exclusive. This is sometimes a problem for me when I am engaging with one of these social groups and they discover all of my identities.

You cannot hide who you are. The only thing that you can hope to do is accept each of the parts of yourself and be proud of what you've become. It has caused me problems before when I have identified myself openly and publicly as a hacker. That is often something that people don't understand or view in a negative light. Still, there would be no point for me to hide that portion of my identity. I have, upon occasion, spent more time explaining what a hacker is than what Fizzmint does in trying to get a new client for my company. (Of course, once they understand that the hacker mentality translates into huge ROI and dollars in their pockets as well as safer personal information and a lower incident response budget, they grow much more enthusiastic.) It used to be possible to hide portions of your identity, to have a professional and a private life. Over the course of the last several years, I have found that the more I try to hide portions of my personal identity from my public persona, the more time I lose. Imagine a company that wants to ask me to join its board. If that board has several very traditional businessmen as members who are startled that I'm a cosplayer at Emerald City Comicon and an old-school goth girl, that company should know in advance who I am and—best case—prepare its board for a new voice. In the worst case, I might spend weeks being vetted for a position into which I would never have been welcomed.

If you are coming out of college, there is no way for you to hide the fact that you were in the College Republicans if you are interviewing with someone who is sympathetic toward the Democratic Party. What this effectively means is that your choices have been limited without you realizing it. The thing people don't keep in mind, though, is that this process has been happening all along.

Save Time by Being You

There are going to be companies that will never hire me. My personal, professional, and public personas don't mesh with their style of corporate governance or the options they wish to have when it comes to their employees. Yet, I am often contacted randomly by companies that have recognized in advance that some part of what I offer as a person or a consultant aligns well with their goals and culture. This is a good thing. What this means is that much of the process of assortative pairing that occurs between a job seeker and a company has happened without you having to go to any trouble. You're saving yourself a lot of work by just being you. And the math is even on my side! Having people voluntarily choose to not contact me because they already know they won't like me saves me time and energy.

Unfortunately, however, there's a lot of privilege involved in being able to integrate your public and private personas. I'm advocating this integration for women in tech specifically, who are in a privileged profession. There are many people who cannot reveal all parts of their lives safely, and I don't want to encourage you to be completely open if doing so will cause you harm. A good example is the very difficult position that nontraditionally gendered people are in when they're not out to part of their social circle. I cannot pretend that I understand what that is like, and I understand that my advocacy of being open is privileged. When I recognize that I'm offering advice aimed squarely at privileged people, my fallback is to offer my help if I can and my ear if I cannot to people who are not able to follow this advice.

In our current social media environment, with people taking pictures of me without me knowing it and posting them to Facebook, I've come to realize that there's nothing I can hide in the long run if I do it in public. I couldn't hide the fact that I occasionally smoke pot, because I've been seen doing it. Plus it's legal in Washington State, lowers blood pressure, and has no calories, so don't judge me too harshly. I'll admit what I do and don't do, because given the existence of urban video surveillance, it's dumb to pretend I'm not being watched. While I have my secrets and confidences, if it's something I've ever been photographed doing at a convention, I don't try to hide it. Yes, sometimes I dress up like a medieval princess or an elven archer, run games at conventions, and play World of Warcraft. Sometimes I spend Saturdays playing poker with my fellow degenerate card players, because it's fun. I am safe in doing so, because my ability to feed myself doesn't depend on people who think that these parts of my personality are repugnant or shameful.

There are parts of your identity that you can keep secret, and there are parts that you cannot. You cannot keep your purple hair and facial piercings private. That is a portion of your identity that you will have to own and accept. You'll also have to recognize that it will limit your choices in some ways. What's important to remember is that you cannot have a personal identity on the Internet that makes you feel happy and comfortable with yourself and also expect that no one in the professional world will not judge you. We rapidly and heuristically sort people in the professional world. Your brand is going to come across whether you want it to or not. The question for you now is if you want to shape and tailor that brand to make yourself the most appealing to the people who you *actually* want to work with, while not caring that people you wouldn't want to work with anyway don't call you up. The irony here is that you're actually going to save a great deal of time in the long run by being open and honest about who you are on the Internet.

Be the Same Person with Your Friends as with Your Colleagues

I still interview for jobs in the technical world. Although I'm the CEO of a startup, I also work with small and large companies on development management and diversity hiring techniques and practices. I am also in the process of giving advice on how to get tech jobs, so I'd better damned well keep my skill set up to date. I am very honest about who I am on Twitter. Like everyone else, I present a more curated visual image of my existence on Instagram. I include every set of skills I ever acquired on LinkedIn. Finally, I leave my Facebook profile open to the public and friend most people even vaguely known to me or my friends. This means that any company that contacts me after doing a simple Google search knows exactly who I am.

This last year, I was contacted by a developer I know. He reached out to me asking if I knew any great candidates for a good contract doing some development management consulting at his company. I mentioned to him that I knew some good candidates and that I might enjoy interviewing for the position as well.

I met with the interviewer from this company. He was a kind and friendly person. About half of our conversation was me asking, "You do realize that I am a . . . ?" Every single time I asked him if he already knew something about me that might be problematic for the position, he said, "Yes, of course." He had already looked over my public profile extensively. He knew that I was the CEO of a startup. He knew I was a hacker and an activist on diversity issues in tech, and he had already thought about whether that would be a problem for his company's clients. He'd seen some of my cosplay photos. It may have been the single best interview I've ever had. Much of the reason for that is the person I was talking to had done his homework. Since I felt comfortable knowing that there wouldn't be any bombs in the conversation, he and I had a great talk. It was so informal because we already knew so much about each other that the questions left over were just those of logistics.

That's where I want you to be. I want your interviews with great companies to be a matter of logistics after they already know they want to hire you. This is why being genuine on the Internet and in real life is so important. I was able to be relaxed and comfortable in that interview because the only real questions left were about whether or not this company and I would be able to create a great project together.

Do you know the feeling of being entirely convinced that someone is being truthful with you? That strong sense that someone has integrity and is being honest? Face to face, it's easy to read that in another human being. Internet searching for someone and seeing a whole person with interests, skills, and a genuine voice is the online equivalent.

BE FINDABLE

Now let's talk about the second piece of personal branding: how to be findable on the Internet.

Hiding Stops Only Recruiters from Finding You—Not Anyone Else

One of the most common problems that recruiters for good companies have is that lots of women and minorities are extraordinarily difficult to find and contact on the Internet. A lot of this comes down to the fact that women are especially closed off on the Internet. I have news for you. If somebody bad wants to find you, they don't need your LinkedIn profile to do so. Public search records will give people anything that they want to know. Not including your email address on your Twitter account and in your biographies on all of your social media profiles won't save you from real-life stalkers, but it will save you from someone who wants to pay you a better hourly wage.

I get questions regularly from women who are nervous about being doxxed (having their personal documents and information revealed online by trolls or harassers). I know where a lot of this anxiety comes from. If a woman has her contact information available on the Internet and something bad happens to her, it's seen as her own fault for having made her contact information available. As someone who has had a police officer tell me that being harassed, stalked, and threatened was my own fault for having my résumé up online, I can tell you that this "blame the victim" mentality is real. But if you don't have your contact information online, you are missing out on jobs and not saving yourself any irritation.

Recruiters are much lazier than stalkers, and you need to make their job as easy as possible for them. At a bare minimum, you should have your email readily available on your personal website or on your LinkedIn profile. If you are someone who is contacted so frequently by recruiters that you want to take your email off of your social media biographies, then your problem is beyond the scope of this chapter, because you're probably well known enough that you don't need the extra help finding jobs—which is an even higher-class problem!

Let Your Profile Picture Do Some of the Talking

Get a professional headshot done. Not the glamour shots, and not the duck-face selfie that was supercute last weekend. Look at the headshots of professionals doing your job with five years of seniority, and follow what you think is the best example. There's a stereotypical headshot of CEOs in tech: it's a down angle of folded arms in rolled-up sleeves and a confident smile. I have that one because it communicates rapidly who and what I am. Go with the tried-and-true; you're not an avant-garde photography artist building a portfolio.

It is quite common for recruiters who are being paid a premium to find diverse candidates for jobs to search for a skill set and a geographic area, such as "PHP Seattle," and to view all of the results, contacting those who look as if they are not white or are female. I cannot fix the system; I can only tell you how I have seen it work. If you are a black woman and don't have your picture on LinkedIn, I think you might be absolutely stunned to find what would happen if you made that information available to potential recruiters. It's not pleasant to know that your gender or ethnicity can sometimes matter when being hired for a coding job, but I'm trying to be honest about what I've seen work for others and for me. I'd also rather work for a company deliberately selecting diverse candidates (even if they're being awkward about it) than one deliberately *de*-selecting diverse candidates.

If You Say You Can Do It, Show You Can Do It

There is a subskill to being findable that many people don't think about. It's this: if you are going to call yourself a web developer, you need to have a website or six up with your portfolio of work. If you say you are a mobile applications developer for Android, I need to be able to find your applications in Google Play. If you are a systems administrator, tell me on your blog about how you manage your own home network with a few cool stories of how you hacked, improved, upgraded, or did other awesome stuff. If you call yourself a social media marketer, I need to see the projects you say you worked on as a top Google search result. The lesson here is this: whatever you say you can do, I had better be able to see samples or a portfolio on the Internet somewhere. Ask yourself this question: What would convince me to hire myself? What could someone see about my work that would let them evaluate my skills without ever meeting me? As tech grows more and more segmented and specialized, people are less and less able to evaluate on their own whether or not you will be a good fit for anything technical or whether you have the relevant skill set. Instead, they look to the Internet to judge whether or not your colleagues and people in your field respect your abilities.

An excellent example of being findable is having a repository openly available on the codesharing site GitHub. If you're someone who loves to code in Python and you're hoping to get a job in Python without necessarily having had one before, then your only real hope is to demonstrate that you can code before you ever walk into a programming interview. If you call yourself a C++ or a Java or a Python developer, and there are no samples available anywhere online of your work, I'm going to have a hard time saying yes to you as fast as you would like me to in a job interview.

BE BOLD

The final piece of advice I have for you is this: be bold. One of the biggest factors contributing to the gender gap in salaries is the fact that many male hiring managers expect to hear from women themselves what their accomplishments are. Women, however, are socialized to be quiet, humble, and unassuming, as we discussed before. This creates a mismatch between expectations and reality.

Compensate for Your Expected Hype Level

People looking for you on the Internet will discount what they think of as your "hype." Hiring managers are tuned and trained to discount a portion of what interviewees say about themselves in the interview process. There is a conflict, however, when women understate their performance and achievements and men overstate theirs. An interviewer who is interviewing a woman may believe that her accomplishments are less than they are, when in reality they are much greater than he understands.

So when I give you the advice to be bold, what I mean by that is simply to be honest about your actual achievements. You may also not yet understand what all of your achievements actually are. As I mentioned in the Applying for Jobs and the Tech Résumé chapter, you need to list every single thing that you've ever done of note in the workplace and every skill you've ever achieved on your résumé. And again, keep updating your résumé every month.

Here's a great example. I was recently approached by a woman whom I'd sponsored and mentored for her first major public tech speech. She asked me, "How many speeches do I have to do before I put 'speaker' in my Twitter bio?" I responded, "Why do you think you need to speak more than once to be a speaker?" I had thought the answer was quite obvious: once you've done something, it's OK to say you've done it—but she didn't have the same viewpoint that I did. I said, "After I had done a single keynote speech, I put keynote speaker in my Twitter bio. Am I being dishonest? How about the people who have 'TED speaker' in their bios?" I think we all have those internal hurdles. I had people telling me I was a hacker and acknowledging me as a good one years before I felt as if I deserved the title and started calling myself one. There is no Ministry of Magic telling you that you've passed your NEWTs and you're a real wizard. Ask yourself what you are stopping yourself from being because you think you'll never be done becoming.

THE LAST KEY

iiyzijfpycplwhpfpppsasupidgvpwtjifxn

THE HACKER
Keren Elazari

When I was thirteen, I really wanted a pair of Rollerblades. I
wanted to be part of the cool kids group, who could blade, in high
school. I was such a geek and a social outcast, though, that even
the group of boys who played Dungeons & Dragons wouldn't let
me join. Maybe it's because I was a girl. True story! Anyway, I spent
my days learning HTML so I could set up a web page (filled with
pictures of the blades I so envied) and logging on to IRC networks
and web forums. This was the early nineties, and there wasn't
as much going on online, so learning how to peer into web servers'
forbidden directories and checking out open telnet connections
to online systems didn't seem criminal. It felt more like exploration
and learning!

Then two things happened that changed my entire life: I
learned how to rollerblade, and at a friend's house I chanced to
see a VHS cassette titled *Hackers*. This 1995 film blew my mind,
because it showed a group of cool kids, intelligent outcasts, who
could will computer networks to do their bidding. And not only
did they rollerblade, they also had a girl! And it was Angelina Jolie!
While I watched her portray the young hacker Acid Burn, I knew
I had found my calling in life. I signed up for computer science
class, started looking online for other hackers in my area, and took
a summer job at the local computer store. I was lucky. My parents
let me have my own computer with unrestricted Internet access.

I had an accessible role model (Jolie). I had a place to learn—at school, at the computer store—and hackers I met at local events took me under their wing. By the time I was eighteen, Tel Aviv saw its first hacker conference. For me, that was the first time I realized hackers were everywhere and that they came in all shapes and sizes (but not genders). I was one of the only women there. A few months later, it was my time to join the Israel Defense Forces (IDF)—as most Israelis do when they reach eighteen. After basic training, I begged my commanding officers to let me work on network security issues. I even went as far as to copy doomsday articles about network sniffing from *Wired* magazine and leave them at the general's desk after getting into his office under false pretenses. Thankfully, instead of a court-martial, I got a chance. Having proven my worth to the IDF, I received the opportunity to join the officers' school and start a career. Fourteen years later, I can honestly say that serving in the army was a privilege—because it provided me with a unique pathway into the dynamic, exciting, and ever-changing world of cyber security.

I learned a lot and became aware of how much I didn't know. Once I even killed a mainframe, a process that wasn't fully controlled or intentional but gave me a rare opportunity to understand the full impact of taking down massive computing resources like that and then getting them running smoothly again. After officers' school I had to figure out a lot about my potential professional future, such as whether I wanted to be a career military woman, take some time for an academic degree, or do something different. These are perhaps complex decisions for a twenty-something woman to make, but I had a very clear compass: I knew I was passionate about cyber security, and in some shape, this would have to be at the core of whatever I did. So I let the compass guide me and signed up for a computer science degree at a local university outside Tel Aviv. I also got a student job on the night shift of a local ISP's network operations center. There, I hoped to learn more about the vast global infrastructures that connected Israel to the rest of the wired world. As anyone who has ever taken math classes after a sleepless night will tell you, balancing computer science with a double graveyard shift four nights a week is not a sustainable effort over time. After a few months I realized a few more things:

1. The Computer Science 1010 math I was struggling to peg down on campus seemed to have little to do with the real-world network-security problems I was working on at my day (well, night) job.
2. Many of the programming languages and techniques we were learning were obsolete and so were the methods used by the crusty professors with unintelligible accents who were teaching us.
3. The out-of-town college I enrolled at had a very conservative, even old-fashioned student life and campus culture, and it wasn't feeling like the best fit for me (perhaps it wasn't the best place for young women in general).
4. I was learning a lot more about computers and networks and security at my night job, and classroom lectures were perhaps not the best place to learn how to code.

My first action after arriving at that conclusion was to quit school for now, telling myself I would move to another college where learning computer science would be more like what I had in mind. I also thought I should take another look at my mental map and compass, and navigate a new route. Just at that time, a friend suggested I interview for an entry-level job at a local consulting firm that was looking for fresh talent with the right background—academic degree not required. The manager I met there the day of the interview deeply impressed me. He was perhaps the most nurturing and thoughtful leader I've met throughout my career, and he was very keen to help me make the most of the job and learn while I took on my first project. However, despite my manager's best intentions and support, danger loomed on the horizon. My first project assignment was to a full-time on-site team of engineers and project managers working on a major security feature inside the operations of the biggest financial institutions in Israel. I was working away from the nurturing embrace of my firm and deep inside the always-cold server rooms and dour basement cafeterias of a very old and conservative organization. The technology I was working on was exciting, new, and promising—it was a system that used a cryptographic concept called PKI (public key infrastructure), which in theory allowed for safer communications, verifiable digital signatures, and greater trust throughout the organization's ecosystem.

The problems happened where theory met with practice. The project hit a lot of road bumps and was always behind schedule. To make things worse, because of the complex nature of the problem, the team I was a part of comprised several subteams from various consulting, integrator, and vendor companies. All of these teams competed for attention and credit from one central manager, who was unfortunately more focused on trying to sell his team members ridiculously overpriced and completely untested new age lifestyle products—he was actually moonlighting as a multilevel marketing guru! As you can imagine, this bizarre situation wasn't something easy to understand or contain for a young woman trying to be professional and successful in her first full-time "adult" job! Rivalries, incidents, and stress were an everyday occurrence.

I stuck to my guns by learning the technology aspects by myself, forging alliances with people who would teach me, and doing my best to have a positive impact on the project. Overall, by navigating these technical and organizational potholes and problems, I learned a lot about the complex technology and business operations that powered almost every financial transaction in Israel. So I still consider it a learning experience, despite its problems. After that first job, I was careful to choose teams, projects, and companies that had the atmosphere and vibe that was right for me—and to walk away when they didn't. Over the years I have learned to identify nurturing managers and team members from the toxic ones, and have also learned that many times, it's fine for me to be doing my own thing or building my own team and that I don't have to always fit in with someone else's concept of what a job and a career is like.

Today, it's strange for me to think of myself as a role model. I always thought of myself as more of a misfit, a nerd, or even a lone wolf, at times. But in 2014 something exceptional happened to me: I became the first Israeli woman to have been invited to speak on the main stage at the annual TED conference. My talk was to be about the positive impact that hackers have had and will continue to have in the future. When I first got the invitation, my initial response (after shock, disbelief, and excitement) was that I was going to get hacked and publicly shamed for speaking up about hackers. This was an inevitable certainty for me. I prepared for it. I made backups of everything. Changed all my passwords to ones so complicated I could barely remember them, let alone guess them. I warned my family about phishing emails and social network fraud. I thought hackers would either be enraged with my portrayal or just paint a target on my head for the LOLZ.

I debated with myself and with others about whether I should wear an Anonymous mask onstage. I intuitively felt that hackers— or anons, anyway—would be upset. Most hackers suffer from an allergic reaction to what they perceive as bullshit. Anonymous, as a global movement or a chaotic collective, is vehemently against personal fame and celebrity, or "namefags," who are people who draw the media's attention to their own person. It's funny: when you consider it, in the hackers' world, it's only good to be famous if you are infamous. And even then it should be under a handle, your nickname, not your real-life persona. If you are known by your real name, it means you got caught. Doxxing (or exposing a target's personal documents—who they are and where they live) is a form of trolling or shaming, and it's been directed at a lot of people who never did anything as public as speaking in front of millions about "good hackers."

I was also terrified of an episode of *How I Hacked Your Mother*: a hacker getting into my mom's webmail account and learning all the glorious details of my dad's ultrasound test and how my dear uncle celebrated his birthday in Australia.

But if I'm being honest, my biggest fear was success. I was afraid the talk would go viral and that hackers might actually watch the talk—hackers who know me by my real name. I was certain they would find inaccuracies or misappropriations or maybe just a typo and devastate me for it. I was afraid they'd call me out as a hacker cheerleader, a hanger-on, or a script kiddie, and throw digital tomatoes at me. Here's a blunt truth: when you put yourself out there, things like that will almost always happen. But I did my best to avoid it and protect myself from such attacks by preparing for those sixteen minutes on the TED stage for months. I chose every word carefully. I vetted and fact-checked every angle, every anecdote, and every story. I chose images and worked with a graphic designer to make sure they really fit the story I wanted to share.

But I didn't do all this work just so hackers wouldn't make fun of me. It was because I realized something: at TED, I was given a once-in-a-lifetime chance to actually hack public opinion about hackers. So today, I see that my job as an academic researcher, an industry analyst, and a public speaker is to hack into people's minds and get them to change what they think about hackers.

It's important to me to point out that while popular media in the past decade have depicted hackers as solitary, often sinister lone wolves or as opportunistic criminals, for me this was never the way of things. Maybe it was because of my romantic nature, the lasting impression of my role model Angelina Jolie in *Hackers*, or just the Israeli mind-set, which prizes chutzpah and cleverness, but I always saw hackers as people who are capable of great things. Heroes, even. But today, most people still tend to overestimate hackers' capabilities but underestimate or misunderstand hackers' ethics and motivations. This can sometimes lead to confused, tragic results. The famous hacker Kevin Mitnick spent eight months in solitary confinement in 1993 because a federal judge believed he could start a nuclear war by whistling into a phone. The brilliant hacker Aaron Swartz, who helped create RSS, Reddit, and the Creative Commons (CC) license, was hounded by the FBI for attempting to liberate academic knowledge. He took his own life rather than face thirty years in prison. So this means that how we see and talk about hackers is not just a case of what people think versus what's really happening. It's even more dangerous than that, because it could lead to shutting down some of the brightest minds of our era. That's why I like to suggest looking at hacking as a crucial form of digital literacy. By analogy, what would happen if we taught ourselves and our children to read and write but discarded the notion of poetry as dangerous and criminal? It's true: some hackers are bad. All hackers operate on a spectrum of choice. And some of these choices may lead to criminal, malicious, or outright catastrophic outcomes. But others will have brilliant, world-changing outcomes—and how we talk about hackers, whether we idolize or demonize them, can determine which outcomes prevail.

We should view hacking as synonymous to innovative thinking and see hackers as I see them: creative, brilliant, daring, and bright minds that stand up for a cause. Anyone can be a hacker and make a difference in the world. This is the story I wanted to share with you.

<MENTORSHIP>

Once upon a time in 2012, I had just completed my first Kickstarter, called LadyCoders. It was to put on and film a seminar teaching women what Liz and I had learned about getting tech jobs as women. About three weeks after the Kickstarter closed, I got an email: "Hi! I like what you're doing with your work on women in tech. If there's a way I can help, let me know." I looked at the email sig, and it said "Jon Callas." I sent back a line: "Is this *the* Jon Callas?" The Jon Callas I knew about was a hugely respected inventor who'd created the encryption for Apple's hard drives and co-founded Pretty Good Privacy with Phil Zimmermann, among other killer stuff. He basically either invented or helped bring to the world most of the encryption systems you and your company use. He sent back his proof pic, and my jaw dropped. If you're a poker player, this is waking up to pocket aces in last position—a.k.a. about as good as it gets. I then sent a gushy and horribly embarrassing thousand-word fangirl email back and asked if he'd deliver the security researcher career track lecture in our weekend seminar. While he's now a dear friend and ally, he started as my mentor and has given me some of the greatest advice of my life. One was particularly relevant as I found my profile growing: "Never get involved in a set of fast-loop replies with someone on the Internet. It teaches them that they're important and you have nothing better to do with your time." The other piece he's had to repeat to me twice.

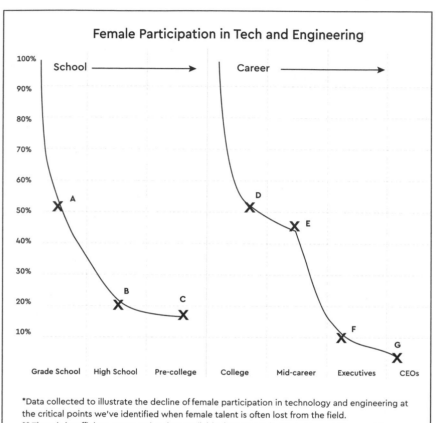

Female Participation in Tech and Engineering

School ⟶

Career ⟶

100%
90%
80%
70%
60%
50% — A
40% — E
30%
20% — B   C
10% — F
                                            G

Grade School   High School   Pre-college   College   Mid-career   Executives   CEOs

D

*Data collected to illustrate the decline of female participation in technology and engineering at the critical points we've identified when female talent is often lost from the field.
** There is insufficient comparative data available, but we are losing women at these points.

Erica R. Melzer, Executive Organizer, WIT Council, @LadyLovesCode

A. Grade School
50 percent of girls aged 9 to 12 feel that engineering jobs are more applicable to boys (Institute of Engineering and Technology, 2015)

B. High school
Women represent 19 percent of all AP Computer Science test takers (US AP Exam Grades Summary Report 2006–2011)

C. Pre-college
15.1 percent of female freshmen intend to choose a STEM major (Higher Education Research Institute's, 2007 Survey of American Freshmen)

D. College
50 percent of first-year female computer science majors left the field in 2003 at U Penn (University of Pennsylvania "Improving the Persistence of First-Year Undergrad Women in Computer Science")

E. Mid-career
44 percent of women remain in their STEM fields beyond mid-career (NCWIT 2010 study)

F. Executives
In 2013, women represented an average of 9.1 percent of board membership in the SV 150 (Fenwick West survey on gender diversity, 2013)

G. CEOs
2.9 percent of the CEOs at Silicon Valley's 138 largest companies are female (Lonergan Partners study, Who Runs Silicon Valley?, 2014)

Once was at ShmooCon when I was rebuilding my Kubuntu Linux laptop for the second time in a month, and the other was about my strong opinions on the cover of this book. In the first case, he told me to just switch to Mac, and in the second, that I wasn't an artist. "You don't have time to be a professional at everything. Stop doing everyone else's job and do yours." You can basically encapsulate an entire career as an information technology professional in those two bits of wisdom. I keep trying to figure out where in the name of George Bernard Shaw he gets his advice.

I've passed Jon's wisdom along to dozens, hundreds of women and minority tech professionals, and I know at least part of the reason he spent that time on me was that he watched me energetically helping others using the resources he gave me.

We don't talk often enough about mentorship, and we should. In this chapter, I'll share some harsh truths, such as the fact that most of your mentor/mentee relationships will fail. And I'll actually spend the greatest part of this chapter on being a mentor, not finding one. The lesson from the story I just told is this: when you have even a modicum of information, start sharing it with others. "Send the elevator back down," as Kevin Spacey once said. The single most important lesson I've learned from Jon is that you don't have to be perfect to be a mentor. I cringe sometimes at giving advice about things I'm not yet perfect at, and I feel like a hypocrite and a fraud doing it. But the alternative is to stay silent and watch people struggle without the information I could give them. I can't do that.

I personally believe that the biggest reason women leak from the pipeline at each point in their tech careers is a lack of mentorship. Imagine it this way: maybe fifty million girls a generation go into STEM fields. If they drop out at each point in their careers at twice the rate boys do, we end up with two Fortune 500 female tech CEOs. If we pour countless dollars into education and the start of the pipeline, and we add, say, 50 percent more girls, at the end we still end up with . . . three Fortune 500 female tech CEOs. Let's plug the holes in the pipe with solid advice, support, and mentorship to solve this problem in reality.

HOW TO FIND A MENTOR

Be Specific and Commit Long Term

Emailing someone and telling them that you want mentorship is likely to get you nowhere, whereas asking for specific help in that person's skill set is likely to get you a response. Over time, getting help and responding with gratitude (and more help) without expectation of reward will evolve into a mentor/mentee relationship. This is closely related to the saying in the tech world about seeking venture capital for a company: "Ask for money, get advice. Ask for advice, get money." Start by working with the person you want to be mentored by, and let the relationship turn more organically into the one you want.

It's a very common experience for people to put effort and time into mentoring someone, only to have the mentee succeed at one task like getting a job and never contact the mentor again. Don't do this! I think of this pitfall as "transactional mentorship," in which a mentor helps a mentee achieve a goal, and the mentee might one day repay the favor if ever in a position to. This is not mentorship. This is someone more junior using someone more senior under the guise of mentorship and trading on what should have been a long-term relationship to get a job or money. Make sure you follow up with mentors to let them know how things went, thank them profusely for their advice, and stay in touch from time to time.

Your Mentors Don't Have to Look Like You

It is a source of never-ending fascination to the people who ask me about mentorships that I have male mentors. How, they ask, could I possibly get advice from a man? Get over the notion that you need to share chromosomes or skin color or age with people to learn from them. This belief stops women and minorities from learning from amazing people. My mentors have almost always been older, well-off, white, cis (I presume), straight (also a strong presumption) men. That's because I'm a CEO of a startup, and I've always been in hugely male-dominated work and academic fields. I need to learn from people who know what it's like to get a startup off the ground, and there aren't enough women who've done that for me to find mentors among them. Also, the men that I develop these relationships with aren't somehow defective in their understanding of my business problems because they're not female. The only real problem I've ever had was explaining to my male mentors why I was having issues none of their male mentees had in certain professional situations—things like not being invited to sit at the table, play poker, or drink scotch with a private group, or not having access to a male-only location where others were doing deals and making company decisions. I always felt embarrassed and was worried that I'd be perceived as whining about not being one of the cool kids, as opposed to calling out real and invisible power structures to which I was being denied access. In every case, I received nothing but support and encouragement, as well as (I assume in most cases and actually know in a few cases) some furious behind-the-scenes conversations with a few of the clueless gentlemen who had caused these problems. It also helps that I'm a fan of good whisky and not a bad card player—it made me an easy "sell." Make it easy for your mentors to help you.

The third thing about mentorship that we don't talk nearly enough about is that the relationship almost always fails. We shake a lot of hands and we do a lot of networking, but the truth is that mentorship is a relationship that should develop much like a friendship does. Just because you get along with many people on a personal basis doesn't obligate you to spend every weekend with them—you pick and choose your friends based on their personal traits and whether you enjoy spending time with them. You'll encounter many people in the professional world, and your mentorship relationships will develop in the same way. You'll find that someone you know gives great advice and seems to genuinely care about your situation. Mentorship is a fundamentally unequal relationship, and if it doesn't work out, there should be no hard feelings. I've reached out to people before who ended up not being receptive to me as a mentor, and that didn't hurt my feelings. Once I sent an email to Travis Kalanick, the CEO of Uber, because I wanted advice on how to find credible advisors in the very industry I was disrupting, and I thought he might have some ideas. He never responded, and I was OK with that. It could be that he wasn't interested in mentoring me, or it could be that he was just too busy. If a mentoring relationship in your life isn't working out or never got started to begin with, let it trail away and die quietly so you can focus on what does help you.

BE A MENTOR

For all of you looking for mentors: Why am I going to spend most of my time on why you should be mentoring someone else? It's because the greatest and best mentors will appear for you if you appear for someone else first. Contribute to your community before expecting anything in return, and you may end up learning more from your mentees than your mentors!

Mentorship is not only a relationship you should seek if you are new to a field. As you become more senior, mentorship of people new to your field is an important component of your professional life, and you should actively seek out these relationships. Notice that I do not say that you should mentor someone younger than you. The only thing you need to know to be a mentor is one more thing than the person you're mentoring. Mentoring someone actually benefits you more than the person you're mentoring. I say that wholeheartedly and seriously; if you have ever taught anyone anything, you know that you only truly learn something when you have taught it yourself. Teaching another person demands a level of understanding, tact, comprehension, creativity, and empathy that most people do not exercise on a daily basis, and will stretch your own abilities, character, and horizons much more than those of the person receiving your advice.

You may be hesitant about revealing your negative experiences, worried that you are too big of a screwup to offer anything of value, or convinced that no one would be interested in hearing what you have to say. You're dead wrong to feel that way about yourself. I was coaching a woman once who was going to do her first public speech. She was nervous about how to get started as a public speaker, and I shared with her a video of my biggest failure as a conference speaker. Even though I know that I did a terrible job, on camera it actually didn't look too horrible. I was able to show her with my own failure that even if you're crashing and burning, most people will never notice. It made a huge difference to her, and I think exposing my own vulnerability and failure helped her even more.

People entering the tech world are absolutely starved for information and personal stories about how to get involved in the corporate work world. They have no idea how to gain access to your world, and you can help them. Many people may have no idea about the simplest things that you know now (even things you learned in this book, like not to use a Hotmail address to apply for a job at Apple, or not to send a résumé in anything other than Microsoft Word when applying to Microsoft, which you learned in the Applying for Jobs and the Tech Résumé chapter!). You may be uncomfortable talking about the problems and missteps in your career to anyone at all. It's common that people who have had a negative experience with a company or field or situation don't want to disillusion a bright-eyed neophyte. They still need your advice. People are going to follow their own paths, and you will not sway them from doing what they want to do. You will, however, give them more information than they would have had otherwise, and perhaps you can help to armor them against the kinds of problems you have faced yourself. This entire book is my attempt to follow my own advice No one can or should pressure you into talking about anything you do not want to, but do consider passing on your experiences to someone who can use the information.

What kind of a mentor do you want to be? Are you someone who is more comfortable working with people on the emotional or intellectual level? You can choose the kind of mentorship you want to provide. No one will ever ask you to give more than you can or should give. You must maintain your own energies, health, career, network, and relationships as you see fit, and if you feel that you would be ideal as an occasional financial sounding board for a tiny startup run by kids who are barely out of their teens, go that direction. If you think that you can handle developing a strong relationship with one or two young men who are becoming team leads in your company and who need to know how to interpret the gaps in the usual woman's résumé, please do so. If you can be a comforting shoulder for a woman who is experiencing difficulties moving ahead in her career due to the roadblocks often placed in her way at her uncaring company, then do so and help her transition to a place that appreciates her skills and abilities. You can only help others by deeply understanding what you are and are not capable of when it comes to handling and conserving your own energy.

There is a direct and nontrivial relationship between you as a mentor and you as a successful career professional. As a mentor, you will gain insight into others, which translates directly into more opportunities in your own career, perhaps by understanding a new market. If you're an entrepreneur, you might see an application in which you may want to invest. If you are a senior software developer who has reached the highest level in your company to which you will ever climb, having strong relationships with some younger technical people who are leaving to start a new company may present an unexpected opportunity. If you are a lead in your section and you can help a junior team member to succeed, you will (or should, in any good company) receive kudos and bonuses for helping to develop employees.

You can and should grow your own network from working with your mentees. They have access to ideas and people that you do not. The number and kind of mentees you should have depends solely on you and your own abilities. Have at least one. Part of your career should be invested in the development of yourself, your brand, and your skills, and part of that development should involve reaching out to others to help, advise, nurture, and learn.

If you are a differently gendered or minority technical worker, you have some strengths that are unique to you. Anyone who has struggled for equal rights and privilege can reach a deep and satisfying knowledge of self that stands everyone well in life. The prize at the end of the road of hardship is the knowledge that your choices are yours and that your life is of your own making, rather than that of the people who made choices for you about who you are and what your life should be like.

It is unfair that further demands should be placed on you, but if you have personally experienced what it's like to be visibly or socially different from a homogenized and unspoken cultural norm, please consider mentoring as many people as possible. Not only is it personally rewarding, but over the course of your life, you will have more connections to others, a more richly developed professional network, and more satisfaction.

Becoming a mentor is nonoptional. You are teaching others something all the time, whether you want to or not. I'll keep repeating that in this book and in my life. With your own example you are inadvertently teaching others what you are like, how to be like you, and how to reach the level you are at in your own career. Take control of those messages and start thinking about the lessons you are teaching to the people you work with and have relationships with. Make a deliberate choice to be an example of a kind, courteous, respectful person who reaches out to people with a helping hand. Your effort will pay off personally and professionally, and you will notice rapidly that others who are not even your mentees will begin to invest you with authority and respect. That respect is worthwhile.

One of the toughest challenges I face is convincing people that their mentorship would be useful. The same social forces that stop women from thinking that they'll be a good fit in technology also contribute to them thinking that their experience is not as worthwhile as others' when it comes to providing advice to new people in the field. They don't realize that their current experience is not only enough but profoundly valuable and unique. As a result, women tend to lose out on all of the benefits of mentorship. Again, the only thing that you need to mentor people is to know one more thing than they know. The vertical connections needed for mentoring and being mentored are vital to being successful in your career.

Here's the last word when it comes to mentorship: there's a difference between mentoring someone and sponsoring someone. Mentors are people to whom you can go for advice and career counseling. They can find a moment or two to answer your emails, and you look up to them for a character trait that you admire and want to have for yourself. A sponsor is someone who is all of these things and has also personally put money in your pocket or gotten you a job directly. Sponsorship is mentorship on steroids. I have had a great number of mentors but only a few sponsors. Sponsorship is a more vulnerable relationship. Sponsoring someone means that you are not just giving them advice—you are putting your name, power, and career behind them. You will face personal consequences if your beneficiary does not succeed. Let's be clear about something: when Sheryl Sandberg describes being mentored by Larry Summers at Harvard in her book *Lean In*, she's actually describing sponsorship. Summers, with his name and reputation, stood behind Sandberg, helping her succeed as an executive and a politician. Sheryl Sandberg has given some of the greatest advice I've ever heard for anyone ever. She gives you the perfect formula for success. Find people who will put their name and power behind you, and then find a way to help them for it. This is not merely a transaction. This is you developing a lengthy, worthwhile, and personal relationship with someone who will, over the long term, make your career and your life better. That's a very personal relationship. Treat it well. Over time, the goal is to turn your mentors and your sponsors into your lifelong friends. These are the people who will invest in your companies, recommend you for jobs, serve on your board, and be part of the rest of your life. Choose them carefully, because they'll become family before you realize it.

THE GAMER
Brianna Wu

I'm about to die, I thought.

The hypothermia kicked in, and I went into convulsions on the shore. It was pitch black, and my glasses had sunk when my boat overturned. Twitching uncontrollably, I focused on the blurry black water in front of me, fighting to stay conscious—knowing I would die if I closed my eyes.

My name is Brianna Wu. I'm a software engineer and the head of development at Giant Spacekat. I am a leader, and I am an entrepreneur. I am also one of the most well-known game developers in our industry. My profile exploded in late 2014 as I stood up to the misogynist hate group known as Gamergate. What I want to tell you about is my life leading up to that moment, the choices that made me who I am today. What kind of person decides to stand up to a political tsunami hell-bent on scaring women out of the game industry?

When I was twenty-one, my first $250,000 startup had just failed, and I was too embarrassed to talk to my friends or family. I didn't know who I was outside of work. And so I wasted a year of my life waiting for the pain to go away.

And it didn't. But that deep entrepreneurial need for adventure had started to flicker again.

Hiding in my apartment wasn't working. Getting lost in video games wasn't working. Wasting my life on Internet message boards and redirecting the anger I felt at myself wasn't working. So I decided to spend the day boating down a river.

The accident came swiftly, overturning the boat and submerging the outboard motor. I plummeted into the icy water, cell phone in my pocket. Thrashing, I swam to the shore as the current swept my boat away. I was lost. Thirty minutes later, as the temperature dropped, the hypothermia started.

The interesting part of this story isn't the rescue, though my tale of being resuscitated in the hull of a boat from the Mississippi Department of Wildlife, Fisheries & Parks is a good one. It's what I decided to do immediately after my brush with death. Taking a taxi home from the ER, dressed in nothing but a hospital gown, I decided life was too precious to waste time licking my wounds. Soon after, I threw away everything that wouldn't fit in my Honda Accord and moved to DC, hell-bent on getting a job in politics.

This is the difference between people who build businesses and people who work for businesses. Risk is something that we accept, something we thrive on. If we don't know how to do it, we build a parachute as we're falling.

Since I'm a well-known figure in technology, people are often surprised that I grew up in Mississippi, the poorest state in the United States. But like so many things in my life, it all happened under unusual circumstances. I was adopted into a family of Mississippians. I never knew my birth mother, but I know I was adopted while my father was getting his medical degree on a navy base.

My adoptive father would often speak of the first job he ever had, working on a farm right out of high school, as if it were a jail sentence. There was a tinge of fear and anger in his voice that terrified me. It was clear that this job was what had propelled my father to be so ambitious. After he got his degree, he left the navy and started a health-care clinic in the eighties, just as the costs of that care were exploding. That small clinic grew into a bigger one and eventually became a network of them. If there's a Republican poster child of the self-made American dream, it would be my father. He was no longer that child doomed to poverty in an economically devastated southern town.

This was the irony of how I grew up, blessed by wealth and opportunity in the poorest state in the country. It would take years for me to appreciate just how much opportunity. The things I learned as a child amounted to an internship many college students would kill for. I would sit with my mom, peppering her with questions as she arranged bank loans. Trips to lawyers were routine, the minutiae of tax code regular dinner conversation. There was a pragmatic "If you want it, get out there and build it" attitude in my house, undoubtedly the greatest gift my parents ever gave me.

A trip to the accountant forever changed my destiny. Frustrated with doing her business's books on paper, my mom arranged to buy an Intel 8086 from the accountant's office. Please understand just how unusual it was for a family to have a computer in the late eighties. Since it was older, our first task was upgrading it to work with modern accounting software. I'll never forget sitting on my mother's office floor with her, figuring out the mysteries of IRQs (interrupt requests) and hard drive configurations. I took to programming instantly—the real world never stood a chance.

But it's important to note that Mississippi scared the hell out of me. Something about the place set every danger sensor in my body on fire. The adults were racist in ways I could sense, even in elementary school. I didn't know what a homosexual was, but darkness in the voices of the people whispering about it scared the hell out of me. Growing up on a steady diet of Rush Limbaugh, I believed with all my soul that feminists were evil incarnate, even as I suspected I was one.

But even though my parents hold beliefs that hurt people in ways they're incapable of understanding, their gifts to me were immense, invaluable. They would give me ambitious technical projects and buy me anything I wanted to make it happen. Install a computer network across a house? Sure. Rewire a car's electrical system? Why not? That kind of initiative is something schools find in kids and stamp out.

In high school, my first attempts at entrepreneurship were less than legal. My turn to the dark side happened when the school administrator came to me as I was working a shift in the library and asked me to store some equipment in a supply closet. I took his keys, promptly driving off campus to have them duplicated. Soon, pilfering boxes of the school's official paper for report cards, I had a booming business.

I first learned Photoshop because I realized that being able to get alcohol was my path to hanging with the cool kids in high school. I bought a very expensive dye-sublimation printer then went to a Blockbuster that was going out of business and bought their lamination machine. Soon I was able to make convincing fake IDs, something that probably would have been a felony if I hadn't been just sixteen years old. I was filled with pride when the winner of Miss MTV Spring Break was a customer from my high school. Her $300 had bought me a sweet 56K modem.

Out of all these ridiculous stories, my favorite is staging a Christian leadership conference. I was seventeen, and I stole twenty sheets of official stationery from my church. I printed letters to all of my friends' parents, congratulating them on their child being chosen to attend the "Presbyterian Leadership Conference, building tomorrow's future Christian leaders." Delighted, they called our school and excused us for a week. We then jumped in our cars and spent the week at a friend's parents' cabin, drinking and doing what teenage boys and girls do without parents.

Ironically, I do feel as if I showed tremendous leadership in arranging this.

I've never had a fear of standing up when others were sitting down. At my first job working at a grocery store as a teenager, I saw a man beating his child with a shoe in the parking lot. This wasn't a spanking; it was a violent beating—blood was gushing from the child's nose. I ran up to the man and started screaming at him to stop, telling him I was going to call the cops. My coworkers were doing nothing, not wanting to get involved. But that wasn't a choice I could make in that moment and live with.

You can read these stories and laugh. And to be honest, as an adult I'm amazed I managed to get through all of this without being hurt or arrested. But I see a child who was unsatisfied with life in a small southern town and decided to go in her own direction. These high jinks weren't about money, which I didn't need. They were really about building something that I wasn't supposed to be able to. And that's a fantastic mind-set for an entrepreneur. We look for opportunities to do something, and then we disrupt.

What you never hear about tech people or entrepreneurs, though, is what I call "butt in chair time." There's a lot of it, and it's not glamorous. Learning the skills that make our work possible is slow and painstaking. When I learned my first programming language, I spent every moment locked in my room for months, hell-bent on just getting things to work—mostly hoping to stop feeling stupid.

I hear from a lot of women in our field that they never feel as if they measure up in terms of skill. While I can't say that I never suffer from this, I do have a lot of faith that what I don't know, I can learn. When I was thirteen, my parents signed me up for a college class for high school students wanting to learn to program. I was terrified going into this, since all the kids were so much older than I was. But to my surprise, I had to drop the class because I already knew everything they were teaching. All those hours learning on my own had given me more skill than I knew.

This supreme stubbornness served me well after leaving college. In my attic is one of my most treasured possessions, a Tupperware container filled with thirty-eight Adobe DVDs. Starting with a copy of Photoshop 4.0, it holds the avalanche of Adobe programs I learned and paid my rent with throughout the 1990s and the first decade of the twenty-first century. Illustrator, GoLive, Flash, After Effects—I picked up the manuals one after another and easily found projects to contribute to.

Late 2010 was the year I decided to go into the game industry. I had been kicking around the idea of either getting a graduate degree or launching a new startup. I signed up for a few classes at my local college, trying to decide if I wanted to commit. Ironically, it was a feminism class that made me decide academia was not something I could stomach any longer. I didn't want to talk about ideas; I wanted to build things in the real world.

A relative offered us the chance to live in my husband's grandmother's house for free if we renovated it. That would free up capital for us to start making a minimal viable product, so I jumped at the chance. I spent half a year renovating the house. Then we moved in, took our rent money, and used it to hire our first employee.

The part of this story that's key is that I saw an opportunity and I went all in. Renovating this house was disgusting and backbreaking. My husband, Frank, and I spent hundreds of hours removing this horrible wallpaper from the forties. I had to wear a hazmat suit and a respirator to encapsulate asbestos in the basement. We had to redo the entire electrical system of the house. But I sucked it up, got to work, and launched my company, Giant Spacekat.

I didn't know anything about making 3-D games in early 2011. So Amanda Warner was my first hire. Amanda was close to my age and had left a job in retail to go back to school and learn animation. My husband had thrown her résumé in the trash, instinctively not liking her girly art style. But I picked it up, saw something in it I loved, and decided to hire her.

Originally, our first game was going to be a top-down tactics game like Disgaea or Final Fantasy Tactics. I loved the original EarthBound, and I thought a tactics game set in the modern world would be something unique. I wanted to make the character classes concepts like party girl, sports bro, and gamer. However, Epic Games came out with the Unreal Engine for iOS, and we threw the entire concept out the window.

Amanda was deeply unnerved when I decided to throw away our plans and make an entirely new kind of game. Amanda is less adventurous than I am—she finds a spot where she's comfortable and tends to stay there. I'd bought a copy of Heavy Rain for a friend who wasn't a gamer, and had seen him fall in love. "I'd always hoped someone would build a game like this!" he said excitedly. "It's about the choices I make, not about mastering a controller with fifteen buttons."

Everything suddenly clicked for me. I couldn't make a company to compete with the multimillion-dollar games for hardcore gamers—my mission was to make games for everyone else. I had a passion for story and animation, but the best story-focused games were extremely complicated. As great as Mass Effect is, the game is mostly a third-person shooter like Gears of War.

Our first game, Revolution 60, shipped in 2014 and was a critical success. The game stars four women from a secret organization called Chessboard who are sent to reestablish control of a space station that's gone off course. Everything goes wrong for them. Revolution 60 is a gorgeously animated four-hour movie about making extremely difficult choices. There is no correct ending. In every one of the twenty-four permutations, you win something and you lose something.

There are so many things about Revolution 60 that I'm proud of, but the accessibility is the biggest one. Anyone can enjoy Revolution 60, gamer or not. The second thing I'm proudest of is how it has feminist overtones. Because all five of the game's main characters are women (the four heroes and one villain), they aren't tokens or Smurfette.

Revolution 60 won three game of the year awards, and as I write this we're about to ship the PC version. I expect Gamergate to make our release a bloodbath, but that's not going to stop me. Our best is yet to come. Revolution 60 was always meant to show what we can do with a design philosophy unlike anyone else in the industry—we have a lot of doors open to us. Right now, I'm working on a multimillion-dollar expansion of our studio.

I have to be honest. Telling you some of my life story is a deeply uncomfortable experience for me. I actually wouldn't recommend many people make the same life decisions I have, because so many of the things I've done have been mistakes, like taking that boat down that river in Mississippi and nearly dying.

But at the same time, there is a fire in me that I don't think all people have. It's a spark, an X factor. Whatever made me stand up to that man beating his child in a Mississippi parking lot is the same thing that made me stand up to Gamergate. And it's the same thing that makes me certain we can make the industry a more inclusive place for women.

If I've learned anything throughout my life, it's that fear stops most people from striving for what they really want. I hope that my story has sparked a bit of fearlessness in you too. Because the truth is that most people make the same choices, settle for the same pleasant distractions, and don't change the world.

We need women leaders, and we need women entrepreneurs who aren't afraid to take chances and aren't afraid to fail. And I promise if you reach inside yourself and find that spark, we'll be standing right beside you as you light the fire.

<NETWORKING and RELATIONSHIPS>

Any IT professional will tell you that the great majority of jobs come from personal connections. The days of the gold pocket watch at sixty-five are gone; it is time to recognize that you, too, are likely to go through a dozen or more jobs before you retire. Maintaining your professional network is realistically the only way that you will find new jobs. Defining the term "professional network" can be tricky, but assume that it means all the people you know in your current field, mentors from college and graduate school, classmates who have gotten jobs at companies that have positions that fit your skill set, friends who have gone into your field or have spouses or other close connections who are top names and personal brands in your field, and over time, the top twenty or so recruiters with whom you have worked.

HOW TO NETWORK

If you're more introverted, you don't have to let that stop you from getting jobs. Staying connected and social can be frustrating to the kind of personality type that is often attracted to tech. We are frequently solitary, focused, dedicated, and single-mindedly devoted to problem solving. This is a job that attracts people who like to sit in one place all day long and uninterruptedly kill bugs and design systems. You are less likely than a typical human to plan your life around the next party and pub crawl, though I've met plenty of techies who put rockstars to shame. Often, keeping up with a social network seems exhausting, pointless, and like a waste of perfectly good energy. Stop thinking of maintaining your professional network as socializing, and start thinking of it as part of your job. Your job does not merely consist of keeping your current job. In this economy, your job is (1) keeping your current job, (2) keeping your skills more current than is necessary for the job you are in and preferably ahead of the market as well, and (3) keeping your network ready for an onslaught of job request emails.

What to Do

Add ten hours a week to your current job, and start thinking of that time as nonoptional professional development time. Use three-quarters of that time to improve your current set of skills by working on projects or your side gig, or taking classes. Use the remaining quarter to build your network. One day the unexpected will happen, and you, too, will find yourself reaching out for the help you have given others.

Pull your network to you. Being surprising and creative helps. If you are uncomfortable socializing or have social anxiety issues, be strategic about the way you want your network to approach you. Developing your blog or social media presence can help; introverts can really shine on social media. It costs little to no social energy to respond to tweets or Facebook posts, and developing a running brand of some kind involving technical humor is one of the best possible ways to keep people coming to you for information, entertainment, and connectedness. Having a reputation for thinking of others and providing useful information to your contacts will spread out past them to the second and third degree in your social network as well.

The Bare-Ass Minimum

I was once asked what the bare-ass minimum amount of networking was for developing those loose ties to lots of people who will get you jobs. After I finished spitting out my perfectly good Earl Grey, I responded with my simple rule: while you are actively job hunting and growing your network, you need to attend three networking events or meetups on a monthly basis.

The first will be your local gigantic meetup. If you're in New York, it would be the NY Tech Meetup. If you're in Seattle, attend New Tech Seattle. Wherever you'll find the greatest number of people in tech at a monthly get-together is the place to be. Your goal should be to get a stack of business cards at least an inch thick and to connect to them all on LinkedIn the next day with a cheerful "Nice to meet you last night at the meetup!" as your hello message.

Your second event will be your skills meetup. If you're a Python developer, you should be attending the local Python meetup to meet and learn from your colleagues. There is no job security in technology, and you have an excellent chance of working with and for many of the people in that room at one point or another. Learn from them, and don't forget to attend the after-party, where people really get to know each other. Your goal at this meetup is to learn about your colleagues, get new skills from the talks and presentations, and ultimately, to speak at that event to present your own original work.

Third, you should attend a mentorship or small group accountability event. This is a group of people in a similar situation as you—perhaps junior developers or program managers or entrepreneurs.

You're there because the people with whom you work right now will not be your colleagues for long. You need to develop strong long-term ties to people who do the same job as you and to be professionally and personally responsible to a group for your career development. This group should be small, confidential, and one in which you all personally know each other. These are the people who understand your work and your struggle, and you should be working hard to help them as much as they help you. If there isn't one in your area, start one.

If you're happy and not actively seeking new positions, you can step back the amount of networking you do and take the opportunity to learn quietly rather than projecting your brand. While self-promoting and learning are both extremely important in your career, they're mutually exclusive activities—we can transmit or receive but we cannot do them at the same time.

Pruning your network is just as important as adding branches and leaves to it. When people you have expended time and effort on and shared inside job tips with let your emails disappear into a black hole of zero response or gratitude, consider gently ceasing to expend effort. This is the same rule that you would follow with your personal friends; when you continue to spend effort and time attempting to contact a friend or set up times together and find that you get a lukewarm or nonexistent response, you eventually stop reaching out and wait to be contacted. Follow the same rule here, but avoid drama or snappishness. Simply stop spending time on someone who hasn't responded to three or more of your posts or attempts at contact and assistance. The flip side of this is the person who may be pestering you with more information than you can possibly use. Often, they are people who may personally know you but also provide career information for a living. Recruiters are particularly guilty of this. If you have someone who is blasting out four job requests a week at you, it is acceptable to stop thanking them or acknowledging their efforts; it is their job to get people hired, and anyone who is indiscriminately taking your time does not need to get more of it.

Recruiters are a special case in your network. Very good independent recruiters are a window into companies and will help you determine your next best step. I think of the very few professional tech recruiters that I trust as being more like talent agents. On an ongoing basis, they'll take a cut of your profits to point you in the right direction, network on your behalf, keep your profile fresh and current, name-drop you in the right places, negotiate for you, and help you make good career choices as you move from position to position. Treat those people as if they are your colleagues, because they are.

Your social network and your professional network will overlap in many areas. A bit of compartmentalization helps; you have a responsibility to other people to use their time well, just as you would have them use your time well and respectfully. Expecting the same courtesy out of the people with whom you interact will help you to maximize your service to your community and the number of jobs for which you will be quietly and privately short-listed.

FOLLOWING UP AND NETWORK MAINTENANCE

One of the biggest gifts new young professionals can give themselves is to follow up with their connections and network. Simply going to coding workshops and tech meetups at coffeehouses is not sufficient; having a plan for how to follow up with a fistful of business cards will ensure that your professional network is healthy and well developed.

There are three main ways that you should be keeping up with your network.

Initial

The first is following up after your initial meeting. Presumably, when you met Ms. X, a creative and name-brand IT professional, you figured out that she had a social media presence on Twitter or Facebook or on her blog. When you return from the conference or meeting, wait a day. Then, contact her via email, Twitter, or Facebook, or comment in an appropriate place on her blog. If she said that she has a preferred means of contact, use it. Do not make assumptions about what other people would want based on your preferences. If she was interested in you and asked you to email her or to remind her of you when you got home, do so. It is common for young professionals to deeply discount the value of mentorship and influence in IT. When someone with social capital takes an interest in you and your work, and contacts you to offer help or a referral, you should enthusiastically and courteously respond. The best possible way to get the attention of a mentor is to ask for help or an opinion. Everyone loves to offer an opinion and will look fondly on someone who acts on this advice, especially if the mentee is courteous, professional, grateful, and nonintrusive.

Ongoing

The second and most important part of network maintenance is ongoing communication. Pick at least one method of touching base at least once a year and keep up with it. Several ways that will work include (1) monitoring your LinkedIn feed for positive changes in your colleagues' and connections' job status (be careful not to congratulate someone over a lateral "promotion" or an involuntary change in employment), (2) collecting the birthdays of all your Facebook friends and using something like Google Calendar to remind you to send a quick happy birthday message to an acquaintance,

(3) keeping a list of the MVPs in your network and tweeting them occasionally with fun information or a question about the restaurants in their area, (4) asking for the opinion of someone with whom you have not spoken in some time on a current issue or code problem, and (5) most importantly, when you see a gig that would suit the talents of someone you know, bring it to that person's attention and, if you have the power to do so, offer to pass a résumé along to the hiring manager. Doing this keeps you fresh in the minds of your network, and you definitely want influential and friendly people to remember you over time.

Thanks

The third way you should be keeping up with your network is by thanking people when they've done something nice for you. There are several levels of appreciation based on what someone has done for you. A good rule on gratitude is that a thank-you card is going to increase the chances that someone will view you positively. A first-class stamp is the cheapest possible way to improve anyone's image of you. Also, it's a good way to practice being kind to people instead of absent, which is something I work hard on in my own life. Use these rules for thanking people who help you:

1. When recruiters or headhunters, whether internal to the company or external (as in a vendor agency or independent recruitment firm) have placed you in a position and you have signed the paperwork, mail a thank-you note to them at their office. This can be adjusted to a nicer thank-you, including a useful gift card, like one for Amazon or Barnes & Noble or a local spa, if they went beyond their job description to get you the job. You can increase that to a gift basket or more if you like. I find that quality dark (nondairy/nut-free) chocolate or an herbal tea gift

set are the best presents: chocolate can be given away for the very few people that do not like or cannot eat it, and herbal tea gift sets work for anyone on earth and can be easily re-gifted (not a small consideration in the world of corporate or impersonal gift giving). Booze is a good present if you already know the person enjoys and will drink that particular kind but not under any other circumstances.

2. When friends personally contact you to tell you about open positions at a company, email, post, or tweet your thanks. If you get the job about which they notified you, mail a thank-you note to their home or office. It would also be nice to buy them a drink or a hamburger the next time you see them. There's no need to expend a great deal of time and effort on this, as ninety-nine out of a hundred of these sorts of informational posts and contacts will go nowhere and have not cost your friends more than fifteen seconds of their time, but you do want to acknowledge and thank them.

3. When a friend internal to a company or with excellent connections there has gotten you hired, been the driving force in getting you the job, and been your reference and champion, and without that person your résumé would never have gotten in front of the hiring manager, you need to thank your friend lavishly. I have had this happen three or four times, and I usually take the friend out for dinner and wine at an excellent restaurant and send a nice gift within two months of my hire date. Possible gifts include a bottle of Dom Pérignon or Cristal or a gift certificate to the opera or symphony. Do not spend less than a tenth of your first month's wages. This is still a tiny amount compared to what can be a bounty of up to a full month's salary that this person may have passed up to jump you past the paid referral system. This person has just personally gotten you a job that will net you tens of thousands of dollars at a bare minimum, and you should express your gratitude thoroughly.

There is a single exception here: if the person has become your boss or is in your hierarchy in any way, you need to give a verbal thank-you and do nothing else. It would be highly inappropriate to present a gift to your new manager or take that person to dinner, and many corporate rules forbid accepting gifts from other employees.

Serve Your Community

Serve your community. It will return the favor. The set of rules I just gave you may seem cynical, but they are really just guidelines for courtesy and decency. Expressing gratitude and interest in others as well as respecting their wishes regarding the way they want to be contacted is the best method to keep your network alive and flourishing. No matter how cutthroat information technology is—and it can be very competitive—the only realistic way to get a job anymore is to have the inside connection. No hiring manager ever wants to advertise on the open market for new hires, because no one wants to go through three thousand résumés and hope to hit the jackpot. Instead, a quiet internal email circulates with a list of positions and a request for résumés. That email is how jobs get filled. Your friends and acquaintances and colleagues are the ones seeing those emails. Be nice to them. Finding ways to be kind to people and stay connected to them as well as advertising your skills is, generally speaking, the way you will get nine out of your next ten gigs.

THE PARENT
Katie Cunningham

I had my son at twenty. I got my first job in tech the same year. This means that during my entire career in tech, I've always had a child.

At the time, I was in school for a BS in psychology. The plan had been to go into special education, a field that had interested me since I was in middle school. In a way, special ed had been an easy choice: I loved reading about disorders, I loved working with the kids, and heck, the praise didn't hurt, either. It was also an extremely orderly plan: get the degree, get the master's, find a local job, work until retirement. Easy-peasy.

Then I was bit by an iguana, requiring three hundred stitches. I lost the use of my right hand for six months, meaning I couldn't attend school.

I was put on heavy meds to combat possible infections, which interfered with my birth control.

Pregnant and feeling like my orderly plan had been ripped to shreds, I realized that I needed a job that could pay well and give me health insurance, since my parents' was about to run out on me. The pay in tech was good. "I'll go back to psych once I have money for grad school!" is what I told myself.

I joined a startup. I liked coding (it was my minor), and I told myself that I could totally get back on track once I was done with this whole pregnancy thing and had saved up a bit of money. I felt like this was the responsible option, and I was desperate to be seen as responsible. There is no shortage of shame heaped upon the woman who is young and pregnant. At the slightest hint of side-eye, I'd launch into my life story, hoping that people would see that I was really quite responsible, that this was just the smallest hiccup, and that my life would be back on track really, really soon.

I clung to the idea that if I could just stick to a plan, everything would be OK. I made list after list, from what I needed to get done at work to what I needed to learn in order to move up to what I needed to do in order to start school again (with, you know, a newborn) to what my husband and I needed for the baby's room. It didn't matter that nothing ever seemed to get checked off. I had a plan.

When I went into labor, the doctor checked me at seven a.m. and told me my son would be born around eleven thirty a.m. He came back a half hour later, at seven thirty a.m., and said it was time to push. I tried to correct him, because he'd said eleven thirty, and now he was messing up the plan. That's how much I craved order.

If there's anything my first child taught me, it was that roller coasters happen and that denying that you're on them only makes the ride worse.

Not long after my son was born, I was laid off, along with 80 percent of my company. In a way, it was a relief, although it would take me years to make that kind of money again. The crazy hours were driving me up the wall, as was the unpredictability of working at a startup. Every week, our business plan seemed to change, and it became more and more unclear how exactly we were going to make money. Postbaby I gave up planning, but I still wanted certainty.

I decided that I wanted something more stable. I considered going back to school to get that special ed degree. It would take some saving, so I got a cushy front-desk job. It didn't pay much, but I could study if things were quiet. I did my homework, and if I didn't need to study, I toyed around with databases and some coding.

At some point, we noticed that the boy wasn't talking.

Some people (mostly family) tried to play this off as no big deal. Einstein didn't talk until he was, like, four! And Cousin Larry spoke late, and look at him now! Perfectly fine! It was tempting to listen to them, as I already had enough on my plate, but the alarm bells wouldn't stop going off. It was his pediatrician who pushed me to get him checked out.

It took a year of poking and prodding and tests and interviews, but at the end of it, we had our first diagnosis: hyperlexia. I was warned that this would probably morph into a diagnosis that would land him on the autism spectrum.

My evenings were now spent doing any number of therapies, most of which annoyed my son. He would grow frustrated with my insistence that he use the right word for something. I would have to fight the rising fear that he might never get better, that he may never respond to the therapy. After a particularly trying night, I realized that, once I had my degree, my workdays would be filled with this as well. Endless IEPs (individualized education programs). Endless meetings. Constant struggles.

I felt my world shrinking. I dropped out of the psychology program and gave up on the idea of going into special ed. I had no idea what I'd be doing, but I knew what my limits were.

My son also taught me the power of knowing your limits, though it would take me years to see that.

At this point, my life was about keeping my head above water. The girl who had once kept lists of lists was now just trying to make it to the end of the day without breaking down. I felt good about deciding what I wasn't going to do, but I felt horrible about the fact that I had no idea what I was going to do instead. I couldn't work a front-desk job my whole life. I probably couldn't afford to keep that job another year, since we were barely keeping the lights on and the rent was constantly going up.

For some reason, I decided to join a writing group. I had no plans to be a writer, but I felt the need to do something to get out of the house, to keep my brain going. I was desperately afraid of becoming dull now that I wasn't in school. My job was mind-numbingly boring but filled with constant busywork, and in the evenings, I found I had little time to just sit and read, since therapies took up every minute from the time I got home until the time the boy went to bed.

I figured that, one night a week, I could indulge in some writing prompts and maybe churn out some silly short stories.

The weird thing about the writing group isn't who I met there but who I met through them. The husband of the person running the group wanted to run a Dungeons & Dragons game. She told me about it, and I convinced my then husband to go with me. There I met the person who would get me an interview at NASA just as I desperately needed to get on a path again.

Being the person who hates ambiguity, I ended up as the person who organized the D&D group. I scheduled our sessions, figured out our dinner orders, remembered who needed to bring what, and even kept notes on our sessions so that I could keep track of what the heck we'd been doing in this Cave of Wonders and Countless Orcs.

The DM (dungeon master—the person who runs the game) insisted that I should apply for a job at the company he was contracting for, and I put him off initially. Me? I worked the front desk at a no-name firm. I was a college dropout. I was a hot mess, wasn't I? He pushed a bit harder, and I thought about how nice it would be not to freak out every time my son's glasses broke, how great it would be to be able to afford a second child, and how awesome it would be to buy shoes whenever we needed them rather than hope that the boy's feet wouldn't grow while we were in our lean months.

I pushed down all my feelings of inadequacy and agreed to an interview.

I'm pretty sure I was brought on at NASA due to my ability to make lots and lots of lists. At least, that's what kept getting emphasized during the interview. I was organized, and that's what they needed: a nerd herder. I became a business analyst.

Though my title stayed the same for the next few years, I started drifting back to coding. It was feast or famine, being a business analyst, and playing around with Python was way more fun than following a project manager around and taking notes.

I'd never really stopped coding, though I'd long since dropped it as a career option. Being laid off only two days after coming back from maternity leave had been nothing short of traumatic. I'd also bought into some of the common misconceptions about the coder life. I believed it was all instability and long hours and crap commutes. I didn't think it would work, now that I had a more realistic view of what life was like with a small child.

However, once I started coding at NASA, I realized that the field was much more nuanced than I'd been led to believe in my college courses. Our hours were reasonable. Layoffs sometimes happened, but we had people who had been on the contract for over a decade. Many of my coworkers had children. Sure, there were shops where everything was crazy and people worked weekends and evenings, but there was a place for people who liked lists and order and clear paths.

It was there that I first began to really believe that I could actually do this coding thing full time, and that it was possible to make a living doing something I loved.

The next shift that came in my life was so slight that I barely even noticed it at first. It came when I agreed to talk at a conference that happened to be in town. Our team's framework of choice (Plone) was holding its yearly conference in DC, and my team had been encouraged to submit talks.

I'd never been to a conference before, and I'd certainly never presented at one. I was so freaked out about the talks that I didn't notice what was happening while I was running around the hallways and chatting with people.

I met people at that first conference who, seven years later, still walk up to me at PyCon and give me a hug. I shook hands with people who, at other conferences, would bring other people my way who I "just had to meet!" I developed friendships that would eventually span the globe.

I was joining a community.

I didn't do it on purpose. I was just trying not to follow my coworkers around (we'd all agreed to break up and meet as many people as possible). Besides, I liked meeting people and talking. I loved talking about what I did at NASA, and I enjoyed looking at all of the neat things other people were doing.

That community, however, became a powerful force in my life. As I became more well known, I suddenly realized that, for once, people were listening when I spoke. People asked me about NASA, about open source in the government, about accessibility, about anything that I could possibly know about. They even contacted me about my son, sometimes to give advice but more often to ask for it.

I felt as if I had been shouting my entire life, but for the first time, I had been heard.

I quickly learned that networking isn't always about the people you purposefully seek out. It's often about the accidental meetings that barely register at the time.

While at the O'Reilly booth at PyCon one year, I chatted up the woman who was doing the vending. She recommended a book to me, and I talked about how another one she had on display had been great for a certain project. We exchanged Twitter handles, and I didn't think much of it.

Some time later, I took to Twitter to complain about the quality of technical writing. The woman (who was an editor at O'Reilly) tweeted back: "Well, why aren't you writing for us?" After some mild panicking, I set up a telephone call with her. Within a fort-night, I had a contract in hand.

That interaction taught me something huge: don't ever dis-count even the briefest of handshakes. Writing my first book led to writing my second book, which led to my third. Those books have reshaped my career in some of the strangest ways, from being invited to keynote at conferences on the other side of the world, to being invited to advise foreign powers on their accessibility laws.

Up until a few years ago, I had very few friends in tech who were women. My coworkers were all men. The people who worked in my area were all men. I wasn't uncomfortable with this, but I also wasn't exactly comfortable. As someone who had spent half of her twenties just keeping her head above water, being slightly uncomfortable felt perfectly fine.

I had made one female friend in the DC area, though, and one day, she called me. She was being asked to start up a chapter of something called PyLadies, but she was insanely busy. Could I help her run it?

I almost said no. I, too, was kind of busy, but she was obviously in a bad spot. We reasoned we could get it spun up, then hand it off. No big, right?

Once again, I had no idea that I was tapping into something bigger than myself.

Within a short amount of time, the number of women I knew in tech doubled, then doubled again, then tripled. I began to feel more and more discomfort at the fact that it had taken so long to meet these wonderful people. I met women just starting out in tech and ones who had been in the industry longer than I'd been alive. I met traditional coders, who had CS degrees, and I met people like myself, who had come from completely different fields.

Most importantly, though, we started trading stories.

My stories about being in tech had always felt singular, as if they were outliers. I never had anyone else's notes to compare them to. Now that I could share stories with others, I realized that others had experienced the same things I had: feeling like an impostor, dealing with the creepy project manager, and getting laid off after having a baby. All along, I'd carried these worries, wondering if it was just me, and now I had my answer: it wasn't. I wasn't alone.

Before this, I had always taken the role of not-a-leader. I'd take notes, I'd give the talk, I'd do the coding, but I never saw myself as someone who might lead or guide. Even when I was a tech lead, I saw myself more as an arbitrator than a figure of power. Here, though, I finally started to see myself as someone who could pave the way for others. I'd started out in PyLadies as a favor to a friend, but I stuck around so that I could make the tech world a better place for the women who came after me.

PyLadies taught me that there's more than one way to be a leader and showed me what kind I am.

<GOING from ENGINEER to EXECUTIVE>

I remember a moment a couple of years ago when I met the wealthy and powerful CEO of a famous tech company. He was someone who thought of himself as an inventor, an artisan, and a member of a team creating a cool product. He was your typical T-shirt-wearing tech prodigy and liked to sit lotus-style on desks when talking. He was speaking to a classroom full of students I'd brought together for a seminar. When one of my students asked him what it was like being the CEO of a big company and having to handle layoffs, he responded by saying that it didn't bother him to lay people off, because it was their responsibility to make sure their finances were handled, and in tech, they wouldn't have any problem finding new jobs anyway. He meant it too. I was looking at someone who had absolutely zero concern for his people and no desire to be a leader. He was an inventor who had had an investment pay off, and as a result he was able to play God with hundreds of lives despite zero leadership training or the desire to be a real leader.

At that moment, I looked at the confusion and revulsion on the faces of the women in that room and realized that this was the model of leadership we in the tech world have come to accept as common, as right, and even as financially superior. This is unacceptable to me, and that moment is at least in part why I wanted to write this book. His statement that people need to look out for themselves is the exact wrong way to build a company founded on mutual responsibility and respect. I've spent a lot of time thinking about what makes a leader, and I've come to the idea that there are three areas of your life that you need to work on to become a leader. Going from an engineer to someone who can manage people and execute the company vision takes a commitment to learning to serve, learning to change, and learning to accept the role.

LEARNING TO SERVE

A leader is a servant to the people around her, and not one of them. At the same time, she is the one others look to for inspiration and guidance. Make no mistake, leadership is a learned skill, not an inborn trait. There are a few near-perfect people out there who have inborn virtue, natural charisma, and moral rectitude, but I am not one of them. I had to set out on the path to learning to be a leader, and I'll spend the rest of my life trying hard to learn those traits that some incredible people seem to have acquired genetically.

Becoming a leader has, for me, been a process of identifying and working on my character flaws. I'm lazy, angry, and arrogant, I speak without thinking, I'm selfish and shallow, I'm quite a glutton, and I don't have much use for people. Almost everything I do now is intended to counter these flaws: I volunteer, help people, try to direct conversations away from me and toward others, get up early to work out (well, most days), and meditate every day on service and joy instead of nursing anger and frustration. I'm a work in progress, but the point is that I'm working on my progress, both in my head and in the world. You are too—but what are you progressing toward?

If I want promptness, kindness, diligence, and joy from the people I lead, I'd better damned well exhibit those virtues in marked excess of that which I expect from others. Otherwise, I'm hypocritically demanding virtue from others based on my power, not on my example.

Virtue: it's an interesting word. I'm using it in the Aristotelian sense; that is, a disposition to behave in the right and moderate manner learned from habit and practice. If you've read about habits, you'll know that they're one of the biggest influences in our lives, and deliberately changing your habits to include service to others is a powerful way of reorienting yourself toward leadership. One of the best CEOs I've ever heard of thought of himself as the support staff for his team. When his team of developers was sick, even though the whole small company was on a deadline for shipping a product, this man showed up late at night with matzoh ball soup and emptied the trashcans full of snotty tissues himself. That is someone who understands that you cannot always control the world you live in, but you can inspire others through your service to them. I think of my job first as being the person who gets coffee for my devs and keeps the lights on. Pride and status get in the way of shipping product.

One issue I've seen people struggle with is interpersonal communication skills. You may be one badass engineer, but if you cannot communicate your purpose and assign tasks to your subordinates in such a way that they're enthused about the tasks you set for them, you can't be an executive. Work on the skill of rephrasing your requests and statements about situations in a positive way. I'm still working hard on this, and I've actually asked people to read parts of this book in advance to help me make sure that I'm phrasing my advice positively instead of negatively. Many engineers are uncomfortable dealing with people. Work hard to lose that discomfort and try to enjoy employing your people skills. Note that I don't say you have to actively enjoy being around people all the time. Dealing with people drains my energy and I need to retreat and recharge.

However, I can always enjoy that I have a skill and that I'm getting better at using it every day.

One way I serve others is to try my absolute best to be a net-positive social media communicator. Lots of people use social media as an outlet for their frustration, but as a leader, the things you say matter to the people you lead. I remember being on the bus a few months ago in the evening as I was on my way to a speaking engagement about social media and personal branding. I saw a woman and a man sitting next to each other in the perfect illustration of manspreading: the situation where a woman is huddled, legs pressed together and bag clutched to chest, away from her seatmate, and the man has both legs spread apart, taking up his seat and half of the seats on either side. I snapped a waist-down picture of the two of them together and composed one hell of a bitingly funny tweet about it. Then I thought about the kind of person I wanted to be and how earlier in the day, a girl had emailed me to thank me for being a role model. I took a deep breath and deleted the tweet. I wouldn't have contributed anything but meanness to the world if I'd hit "Send." Sure, I would have scored some short-term humor points, but that's not who I want to be.

You're also now a representative of your company. Start assuming that everything you say online will be read by your mom, your boss, your potential descendants, and a background check officer at a federal agency (which isn't far from the truth anyway). I recognized some time ago that anything I say on my Facebook, LinkedIn, and Twitter profiles would be discovered anyway, and I opened them up to the public. I figured that I might as well keep my lack of privacy in mind rather than trusting privacy controls on social media sites I don't own and web services for which I do not pay. You no longer get to bury your head in the sand when it comes to social issues. You can be yourself on social media, but you cannot add "views are my own" to your Twitter bio and pretend no one from your company is watching. I talk a lot on social media, but I don't complain about people at restaurants or coffee shops anymore, no matter how bad the customer service was. A lot of people listen to me now, and as a representative of my company, I have to be mindful of the image I'm presenting.

The last part of learning to serve others, and the hardest lesson I'm still working on, is this: don't be the smartest person in the room. That's a direct quote from a mentor and former CEO of mine. Humility is an especially hard lesson for me to learn. As a female engineer, I've been screaming for my entire career that I'm right, that my code is good enough, that my solution works, and that I belong in this room with the rest of the engineers. I've had to shift my approach a lot. Now what matters is that the people who I'm talking with feel as though they're heard, not that I'm smart. That is how I can help build consensus on the right way to solve a problem. If you figure out how to do this, please tell me. I'll report back in about twenty years and let you know how this particular journey turned out.

LEARNING TO CHANGE

There's an uncomfortable truth about transitioning from being a team member to being a leader that I've been grappling with for a long time and that you'll want to prepare yourself for as well. You can become a leader, but it will set you apart from some of the people you have close relationships with now.

This is a difficult thing to talk about, because it's about social class, judgment, and your own goals. Professional athletes and musicians who came from less privileged backgrounds often will struggle with negative influences from the people who loved and supported them while they were on the way up. I have friends and dear loved ones who have loved and supported me but are still fighting to give up drugs, get out of prison, and get their lives together. I can love them and be there for them to the best of my ability without being pulled into problems I have no power to fix. Think very hard about the people you surround yourself with. The motivational speaker Jim Rohn famously said that "you are the average of the five people you spend the most time with." I choose to be around people whom I admire as well as like. I surround myself with people whom I respect for their kindness, entrepreneurial spirit, irrepressible joy, courtesy, intelligence, and strength, and then I figure out if we like the same comic books and TV shows. Those are the people I try to spend my time with. A large number of them are in the acknowledgments to this book.

If you're a developer or an engineer, you're probably used to your project managers and bosses communicating with you and around you in ways you may not even notice. As an IC (individual contributor), you are benefiting from the more people-savvy communicators in your organization. When you move into your first management position, you'll realize that developers and engineers are often allowed to be much more eccentric or difficult than managers, simply because there's no need for them to develop those skills. I remember an email I once wrote asking for an accommodation for my disability (I have degenerative disc disease, which causes me issues with movement and stationary work). I had the good sense to pass it through my project manager at the time. She helped me see that telling upper management "if you expect me to work under these conditions, you're sorely and stupidly mistaken" might not help me achieve my intended purpose as effectively as "I'd be so grateful if you'd help me reach my potential when it comes to my output in service to this organization." You'll start to be the person who helps your developers and engineers communicate effectively, which means you'll need to learn to do so yourself. Teaching a full set of communication skills is beyond the scope of this book, but when I wanted to learn, I began with Dale Carnegie's *How to Win Friends and Influence People*. People often discover Carnegie's world-famous book just as they're ready to really hear the message in it: service to others is the same thing as service to yourself. I wouldn't have been ready to hear that message and really believe it until I had come to the realization on my own that I lacked communication and people skills, and that I was the one who needed to change.

If there's any one thing I can tell you about changing yourself into someone others will respect and give leadership tasks to, it's this: start making a habit of being on time by being early. People who are habitually punctual usually have a whole lot of other life skills nailed down. They manage their time well. They're honest with themselves about how long tasks will take. They have the logistics of their city and transport down. They respect you and your time. They have built time into their day for small tasks, often after they've arrived early to meetings. They likely sleep and eat on a healthier schedule. Sometimes you cannot help being late. There's a difference, however, between someone whose definition of "on time" is five minutes late and who arrives more than fifteen minutes late half the time, and a person who arrives early or on time nineteen out of twenty times. Habitually late people are not honest with themselves about their commitments and how long their daily tasks will take to execute—or they're pushovers about letting others dictate their schedule. That's not someone I want managing others. The more time I spend with the people who run companies, the more I realize that this is one of the unstated expectations for leaders. When I set up coffee with fellow CEOs, they are nearly never late. That's even in Seattle, which has a truly terrible transportation system and which can unexpectedly jam up with hours of traffic and overpacked buses and trains. The day Kristin and I met at a café to work on her The Educator chapter here in Redmond, Washington, was one of the worst traffic days in years. Dozens of collisions and jams locked up every part of Seattle within a twenty-mile radius. She was ten minutes early to the café off the legendary-for-gridlock State Route 520, beveraged, fresh, and prepared to work (I got there two minutes earlier, which means that I won). When leaders say they'll be on time, they make it happen.

Develop your personality and interests outside technology. I have lots and lots of interests, side projects, hobbies, and fun things I do. I have to, or I would be a deadly dull person with a stultifying lack of stories, points of commonality, and conversation openers. At this point, it would be accurate to call me a serious limit Texas hold'em poker player. I like listening to audiobooks, and I ran a Kickstarter to bring Frankenstein's creature's favorite book, Volney's *On Ruins*, to audiobook for the first time ever. I helped found Hack the People Foundation to provide mentorship to underprivileged technologists. I founded InfoSec Unlocked to help underrepresented hackers propose conference panels and talks. I take cat pictures, play guitar, read, play World of Warcraft, do triathlons, and cook. If you don't have a cool hobby and some volunteer commitments, you'll miss out on personal growth and contributing to your community. There's likely something you always wanted to try but never have. One day, I'll get up the courage to bicycle in a velodrome at that crazy forty-five degree angle, and I keep meaning to learn to play cricket. Developing yourself outside your profession is the key to being a well-rounded person who can connect with others.

There's a side note I'd like to add here about the value of some of those outside hobbies when it comes to networking with business and technology leaders. In the 1980s, women were often encouraged to learn to play golf so they could join in business deals on the links. I'm not really a golfer, and most of the techies I know aren't, either, but there's a solid side culture in technology of people who love to play poker, and I've made some great connections over the poker table. I would play anyway, but I can use some of that time that I enjoy to attend tech charity poker events and teach some great women in tech to play poker as well. If you have a hobby you'd do anyway and are open to sharing with and teaching others, consider starting an interest group. I started (to the best of my knowledge) the only C-suite ladies' poker game here in Seattle, and I've had a wonderful time connecting and playing. I know other techies who bike, sail, play music, and more together, and they love it!

LEARNING TO ACCEPT THE ROLE

Women are often uncomfortable acknowledging that they have power and authority. I saw an extraordinarily clear example in 2013 at a Seattle tech networking event called Founder Friday at the local Facebook offices. It's an event put on in multiple cities by the amazing people at Women 2.0 (which contributor Angie Chang founded!). The goal is to allow women in technology to network by creating a friendly space and relaxed atmosphere with notable speakers.

It was a networking event, so I clutched my better-than-usual-grade Riesling and started the business-card-shuffle in the pregaming part of the evening. There were maybe twenty-five women there, and I introduced myself to the nearest person I saw.

"Hi! I'm Tarah Wheeler Van Vlack, and I'm the CEO of Fizzmint, an employee administrative task and compliance management company. What do you do?"

"I am part of a cool startup that does X."

"Oh really?" I said. "What do you do there?"

She blushed. "I do the business stuff. My co-founder, he does all the technical stuff."

"Wow, that's awesome! What do you call yourself there?"

"Sorry," she said. "I'm just the chief cook and bottle washer. My co-founder, he's an awesome CTO."

You have a technical co-founder, and you handle all the business, marketing, hiring, and tax matters. What else could your title be but CEO?

I moved on to the next person, thinking that this might be an aberration. It's really, really not. Out of twenty-five women at the event, I met two people who had a C-suite title on their business cards. Yet every one of them was a co-founder of an up-and-coming startup.

We know the insidious, vicious effects of impostor syndrome. I won't pretend that I don't feel the impulse to soften my speech, to not intimidate the people to whom I'm speaking every once in a while. When you do an image search for "CEO" on Google, the first woman who appears (about a hundred images down) is CEO Barbie.

Don't push your authority and power away. It doesn't "soften your image." It makes you powerless and ineffectual. Have the respect for the people you lead, like it or not, by accepting that they trust you and that it is your obligation and joy to learn as much as you can to serve them as best you can. This is another dangerous moment in the women-in-tech pipeline. This is the moment where the narrative about women serving and men leading can take over in your head and make you default to the socially acceptable role of behind-the-scenes service, rather than out-front inspiration. I have some comforting news for you. The only people who don't suffer from impostor syndrome are actual impostors. Not knowing what to do next is a side effect of living an exciting life where you can have a real impact on people who, if in your place, would have equally no idea what to do next. It is not a symptom of being stupid or of having poor leadership abilities. If you don't know what else to do, change the narrative. Think of a strong leader you admire, and do what you think he or she would do in your position. Really think it out. It's OK to use a fictional character. I sometimes very seriously ask myself what I think Captain Picard or Janeway would do. Listen to music that makes you stand up straighter and want to win before walking into a room full of people you have to lead. Yes, you're making this up as you go. So are all the rest of us.

You're going to start making decisions on behalf of other people. This is one of the hardest parts of leadership. I often ask myself: What gives me the right to decide for other people what is right and best? Only a strong sense of self and thoroughly thinking through *why* you make the choices you do will give you a strong foundation on which to build your internal decision-making apparatus. I base my decisions on my ethics and on expected utility, what I believe to be right and what is likely to be most effective. Then I constantly reevaluate the effects of my choices to tune that process. I don't generally second-guess myself; I believe that I make the best decisions I can with the information I have at the time, and I try to leave those choices in the past while still taking their effects into account as I make future decisions. A leader's job is to make good decisions about everything from which pencils to buy to which vision of your company to embrace. Whatever your framework for decisions is, include both ethics and practicality, and constantly refine. It's how you can be effective and still be able to look at yourself in the mirror at the end of the day.

Develop your sense of judgment about people to the point that you've learned to trust your instincts about someone's character. I screw up sometimes, and I make mistakes all the time. However, we have built a culture at Fizzmint that ultimately reflects my personal decisions about people's characters. You are going to start learning to consciously harness the judgments you make about people, because if you don't, you'll judge unconsciously. That's how poor hiring decisions get made, like hiring a team of nothing but straight white men and thinking it's because they're the only ones tough enough to stand up for their coding choices. Without examining how you judge others, you'll behave reflexively and reactively. Don't not think.

This choice of leadership as a life goal is a solitary one. If you can joyfully accept some isolation in exchange for a big life, you may want to start on the path. No one can walk with you, but there are always people to help show the way.

SELF-CARE FOR LEADERS

Earlier today, May 7, 2015, I actually walked out into traffic in downtown Seattle. About three hours ago, I finished running a quarterly board meeting for Fizzmint. After that, I knew I should leave the office, because I'd already worked for about ten hours, so I walked from South Lake Union to downtown Seattle and muddled about Pacific Place, a shopping center. I realized I hadn't eaten in at least six or seven hours, so I sat down at a conveyor belt sushi joint and promptly knocked the soy sauce all over the table. It turned out that my hands were shaking from low blood sugar and stress. I ate a roll or two, then thought about going to see the movie *Kung Fu Killer* with Donnie Yen. The fact that I was too tired to go and decided to head to the bus stop should tell you something—I never miss a Donnie Yen movie in theaters. Walking to the bus stop, I was so oblivious to what was happening around me that I walked into the intersection of Seventh Avenue and Pike Street against traffic. I didn't even realize I'd done so until a car swerved around me and gave me a Seattle Salute.

There's some irony in the fact that right this minute at 9:32 p.m. on May 7, 2015 (while I should be drinking tea and sitting in a bathtub, congratulating myself for not dying and also running a good board meeting), I'm writing what is less a segment in this book and more an open letter to all women at a certain point in their careers. You're about to get a big old truth bomb from me on self-care.

As technical women, we're used to being and are even self-selected to be very self-reliant, fine with working alone for long periods, and less often required to be people pleasers and public performers. At this point in my career, I'm transitioning into someone who is less a technologist and more a people person by trade, if not always by preference. I didn't realize this, and many of you won't have realized it, either, but this is very, very hard physical work. The physical and mental muscles and skills you're going to be using are different than the ones you use to develop code, and you need to take care of your body and mind the way you would if you were an athlete. I drank black coffee today instead of eating small protein meals. I didn't plan the loss of my commute time when I made my agenda today. I thought I'd be fine to keep working after a big meeting that I had to run with all my senses and brains engaged. I almost murdered the nice saleslady at Nordstrom for bothering me while I had sunglasses and headphones on. My hands are still a bit shaky even as I'm typing this. I was an *idiot* today.

Hey, y'all! Watch me do a little self-care right now. Now that I have the story of what happened today down on paper (metaphorically speaking, since I'm typing very slowly), I'm going to take my own good advice and go away from my computer and rest. I need some mochi, *Cowboy Bebop*, and laser-pointer time with my kitten.

WHAT DOES THE PYTHON SAY?

xidhgnmptjimrhbleefeirucqemejfegixpbimetoh
oepbxkuwmesqokrgkblemwiipcmexctxsronelqoiu

THE CRUSADER
Angie Chang

I was born and raised in middle-class Orange County on the western coast of California to immigrant parents from Taiwan. As immi-
grants, my parents were determined that my sister and I would
have a good life of exploration, education, and stability. This meant
that when we were children, my mother enrolled us in many rec-
reational activities inexpensively at the local community college
or park, discovering quickly our excitement for (or sheer lack of
ability for) dancing, tumbling, martial arts, softball, tennis, geode
cracking, and more.

We were also enrolled in Chinese school on Saturdays (where
we had an hour of activity, which varied from modern dance
accompanied by Janet Jackson's "If" to shooting hoops to learning kung fu) and were members of the local Girl Scout troop (my
mother said it would "look good for college"), which surprisingly
built a lot of grit for us as annual cookie-shills at the local super-
market. The Silver and Gold Awards were surprisingly easy to
achieve—you had to earn a number of badges, and you were
recognized by troop leaders at an award ceremony with candles
and ribbons.

The Girl Scout camp booklet mailed to my house revealed an
opportunity to be a summer camp counselor at Camp Juliette
Low, a camp for disabled girls, and after I was waitlisted, I was
accepted to become a counselor at a different camp in Kansas

for a handful of seriously disabled young girls. I wrote my college admissions essay about the experience and was accepted into every University of California school I applied for, but I didn't reach for Stanford or MIT, as my mother had hoped.

A helicopter parent, you might say accusingly. But my mother didn't hover—she simply enrolled us in and drove us to many activities to try things that we came to like or not like. The only extracurricular activity I was not allowed to drop, despite all my protesting, was the piano lessons. I could set the oven timer to sixty minutes and plop down on the padded wooden chair in front of the ivory keys and silently protest for an hour that I was forced to sit there, or I could slowly wind through Bach and then warm up with Beethoven, finishing with some tricky favorites by Mozart and Tchaikovsky.

My mother's rationale for my years of piano lessons was pure strategic thinking. She reasoned that piano teachers are paid in cash, teach in the home, and can easily make a living (tax-free) in the suburbs. I joke now that my mother knew the sky-high rate of divorce today and was setting us up for financial independence from an early age. She herself is a younger daughter in a large family from central Taiwan—the family swung on the pendulum between poverty and wealth her entire life. My mother as a young child was almost left in the mountains with another family because there were too many mouths to feed, and then in high school she had a private chauffeur to drive her to school. In the patriarchal society that was Taiwan in the 1950s, she was often shortchanged when my grandfather handed out financial rewards to his three sons and ignored his five daughters. My grandmother was a quiet supporter of my mother, helping her out financially on the side as my mother moved to the United States in search of a new life. My mother's penchant for preparation and not depending on another (often male) partner for financial support was ingrained early on and passed on to my sister and me.

The one extracurricular activity my mother did not pressure me to sign up for was a technology class. My family purchased a computer and modem when the Internet was a household item in the 1990s, but she discouraged tinkering (you might break something, God forbid) and scolded my sister and me for indulging in AOL chat rooms late into the night. Little did she know she had supplied me with a creative outlet I took advantage of to learn to create my own websites.

In high school, my friends—including my sister—were outgoing, charismatic girls who led clubs and organizations. To this day, quiet comes with a negative connotation, and this was the word often used to describe my personality. I enjoyed team activities like softball, cross-country, and track but didn't need to be the center of attention or the loudest voice in the group. This meant that I was perfectly fine being the supportive friend who drove others around in my car for volunteer activities and project meetings.

And in the nature of being supportive, I helped make websites and newsletters (both online and print) for my friends' clubs. I took pictures and learned to use Photoshop to crop and enhance. On my personal computer at home, I created lists of the clubs' current activities, successes, needs, goals, and calls for involvement that could be distributed in person or online to the club members. For the website, I studied other clubs' websites and built one of my own with simple HTML and CSS. I started hand-coding my very simple blog in 1999, noting pleasures such as discovering Fair Isle sweaters on the cold East Coast and sharing favorite lines from books like *Perks of Being a Wallflower* or *The Melancholy Death of Oyster Boy & Other Stories* by Tim Burton.

I identified as an emo kid—a bit of an outsider—when I was younger, and when I got to University of California, Berkeley, I joined the entertainment group on campus. We put on concerts and movie showings—we were interested in bands like Ozma and creepy Todd Solondz movies. I become the webmaster for the organization, as others could help design and put up flyers, but I could update the website with our bookings. I realized this was something people would pay for.

My next-door neighbor Cody in the residence halls at UC Berkeley was a math and computer whiz, motivated by the Caltech rejection letter he pinned bedside for all to see. He was also my friend and encouraged me to apply for a job at the computing center as a web designer. He assured me that he would refer me and that I was qualified. I didn't get the job the first time I applied, but I got it the next time he told me the job was available again and started getting paid an unheard-of $15 an hour to be a web designer for the residential computing department of UC Berkeley. This job beat the $5 an hour gig I previously had sitting at the register at the student arcade and the stipend I received for being webmaster at the entertainment group.

Cody was also studying math and computer science at UC Berkeley, and we walked to lectures together. I had taken a class in computer science in high school and liked it, so I figured my college classes would be easy. I was dead wrong. I immediately gave up on Math 1A at UC Berkeley, because I was on track to fail after a month, and subsequently never took a math class in college again. I also barely made it through two computer science prerequisite courses (CS3 and CS61A) before deciding that learning the antiquated programming language Scheme to solve card puzzles was not something I could succeed at.

I had thought my dabbling in making websites could easily translate into being a computer science major at UC Berkeley, but as I was on track to receive some Cs in my computer science classes, I withdrew from them or took them on a pass/fail basis to avoid lowering my GPA further. I longed to join my friends in lab to share their excitement, but after building a compiler in the first year of class and feeling lost in my first electrical engineering class (EE42), I decided to throw in the towel and just focus on being able to graduate from UC Berkeley. I decided to major in English, because I didn't fear writing at length, and then tacked on a social welfare major to my degree. I enjoyed learning about how government programs support Americans with average or below average incomes, because growing up in conservative Orange County, I didn't learn these things.

I graduated from UC Berkeley in 2004 not feeling like a sparkling, successful human being. My social welfare professors kept telling us that social workers experience burnout in just a few years, and while my mother was optimistic that my English major would make me a fantastic secretary to a glorious CEO, I was not really very excited about being a secretary.

I went on Craigslist to look for a job. Craigslist is a super fun place to discover things, like a whole bunch of jobs I didn't know existed. I didn't know what a brand-naming company was, but I worked at one for a few weeks until I realized that it wasn't my jam. I met some odd people in my job search who were looking to hire for some questionable roles (and for me to accept the job offer on the spot—no way!). I walked into some very large gleaming buildings, hoping one of the tired-looking hiring managers who found my résumé at the bottom of their database would offer me a tech job.

The one interview that I walked out of feeling interested in learning more about the job was at a startup in Palo Alto. The guys had just received venture funding and were excited to grow their team. I would be employee number nine and a web producer on the engineering team. Their excitement was palpable. I got the feeling the interview was more of a culture fit, not a technical interview. The founders and I got along as people. We shared energies in different ways, and I got the job offer. The mistake I made was naming my salary based on the average salaries of social welfare workers, so I got that. I heard later that another guy who interviewed for the same job asked for $70,000 a year and would have gotten it if they had decided to offer him the role, but they gave it to me instead. I took less money, and I didn't know until later what I had done.

Regardless, I was excited to join the small team in Palo Alto and was introduced to Silicon Valley, a place I had heard about before but whose importance I hadn't fully understood. I attended some conferences and events on the Stanford University campus with coworkers and friends, all focused on entrepreneurship, new technology, and venture capital. New to the area, I joined Meetup.com and attended events to learn about the wealth of Web 2.0 startups created by technologists.

In a short while, I was tired of being pitched car parts websites, tech products for tech startups, and yet another bland version of this for that. One of my startup's co-founders, the then CTO of the company, recommended that I think of my own ideas, because as one of the few women at these many tech events, I could imagine different markets and solutions.

I imagined websites that could appeal to a broad market. I wanted a Yelp for beauty products, because I could never figure out which mascara or product on the market was the one for me. So with the help of friends, some of them developers and some of them not, I built an alpha version of this website, and fingers pointed at me to raise venture capital (VC) funding for this project. I assumed the position of CEO for the project and took $5,000 from friends and family to write a fuzzy business plan, create a pitch deck, and start presenting at VC firms. We failed to secure VC funding for the project, but in the meantime, my insistence on finding and meeting the few women in the technology field in Palo Alto yielded me the women who would become my co-founders of Women 2.0.

We called it Women 2.0 because we wanted to know where all the women were in the next iteration of the web. I created the logo from the Web 2.0 logo that year—but in place of the word "web" we put "women" in pink. That hot-pink hue haunts me a decade later. I hosted monthly Women 2.0 meetups at my rented Palo Alto Eichler home, where we served inexpensive wine from Trader Joe's and shrimp cocktail from Whole Foods. Women heeded the call, and we met monthly to discuss our current jobs, our dream jobs, and our ventures.

The first Women 2.0 Conference was in 2006, and a hundred women and a few men participated. We asked women we knew had raised funding for their companies or projects to participate onstage and used them as the marquee names in our marketing. We knew venture capital was a man's game, and we celebrated and applauded the women who had successfully navigated that minefield.

My co-founder and the CEO of Women 2.0 studied business as an undergraduate in Canada, so she incorporated a business-plan competition into our annual conferences, along with a live pitch in front of investors for prize money. Our annual event grew yearly, and our meetups became more formalized.

Over the years, my Women 2.0 co-founders and I switched jobs and moved to new cities, but we always worked on Women 2.0 on our nights and weekends. We believed in the community of ambitious women interested in entrepreneurship and technology that we had built, and I kept an email list of our interested members. Women 2.0 became my ad hoc way of learning marketing.

During the day, I worked at tech startups. I left my first startup job for another after a year, and then I was laid off from that job after six months. I moved to San Francisco for another job to be a product manager (leaving the engineering world), and the economy took a hit the week I was laid off from that role.

I also realized that Women 2.0 was limiting, because few women identify and declare themselves as entrepreneurs. I was looking to attend a Girl Geek Dinner in the Bay Area and couldn't find the local chapter, so I started the Bay Area chapter of Girl Geek Dinners. Google had hosted a Girl Geek Dinner in London that was attended by several dozen women, so I asked around for the right contact at Google to host a Girl Geek Dinner at their headquarters in Mountain View, California.

We opened registration for the Girl Geek Dinner midweek, and I posted the event to Facebook and sent a few emails. Over the weekend, the event had spread through word of mouth, and come Monday morning the Google staff were astounded to find that over four hundred women had signed up to attend. We quickly closed registration, as four hundred was the capacity for the biggest space at Google at the time. Google delivered their promise of a Girl Geek Dinner, renting large white tents and supplying unlimited sushi and "Google Girl" mugs to all who attended. Google's girl geeks wore their fun branded T-shirts at registration and mingled with the crowd. The event was a rousing success, and the panel featured a variety of women from VCs to entrepreneurs to a Google executive to a startup CEO who was eventually acqui-hired by LinkedIn.

I have been in and out of technology jobs (either because I was laid off or because I moved on) and spent vast amounts of time being unemployed, but surprisingly enough, hosting events that companies sponsor and pay for made me feel like a successful human being. I was asked to give a welcome speech at every Girl Geek Dinner I co-organized with sponsoring companies, and women started viewing me as a leader. My name was associated with emails sent out about events, and recently I was at UPS and gave my name, and the girl at the other register said, "You're *the* Angie Chang of Girl Geek Dinners!"

Similarly, my side project Women 2.0 was gaining traction, and I was updating the website and sending emails about events and updates to thousands of women. At one point, I decided to open up the Women 2.0 website (formerly used for event announcements and business plan competitions only) to share female founders' stories of going from idea to launch, or from idea to VC funding. Our WordPress content management system was ripe for this, and our website traffic started climbing and our mailing list grew in popularity as the content platform grew.

The last job I had that I interviewed for was to become a product manager at an education startup in San Francisco with venture funding. I only took the job because I wanted to pay the rent. My ex-boyfriend would disagree with this statement, because I wasn't paying rent at the time (I was living with him), but I wanted a job so that I could feel normal in the recession. Having a job gives you a sense of who you are, and I was determined to be a product manager—a mini CEO.

The job itself was average, which made me aware of my lack of interest in doing anything at the job—I wanted badly to continue sharing our female entrepreneur stories all day on our platform and to inspire women to break the mold and start companies, venture forth, raise funding, grow huge, make money, take board seats, and so forth.

After a year of warming a seat at this education startup in the engineering/product management department, I was laid off when it was acquired by a larger education company, and somehow my thirteen months of service didn't qualify for the one-year cliff for options (due to a three-month probation they added before vesting started for employees). I was pissed. I was also very glad that I had Women 2.0 on the side, because my co-founder had also in the last year started strongly considering working on Women 2.0 full time.

Together, we made a plan for success on our own terms, and we were ambitious. We wanted our conference to attract a thousand women, instead of our usual two hundred attendees. We would charge market rate, because we became our own full-time employees, and I became editor in chief of a media company. We grew our staff in San Francisco, entered new markets in Latin America and Europe, executed on the thousand-woman conferences, and became the defining voice and brand for ambitious women in entrepreneurship and technology. My co-founder (Women 2.0's CEO) and I were recognized in *Fast Company*'s "30 under 30" in 2010, and I became really good at producing three high-quality content items a day about female entrepreneurship, ambition, and technology. Our weekly email newsletter was chock-full of useful content for women, and my editor's note at the top helped define each week's focus, so I got credit for publishing so much content on the web. My content was syndicated by *Forbes* and the *Huffington Post*, and I dabbled with the idea of contributing my articles to larger publications as well.

All said and done, I made it through one year of full-time work as official editor in chief at Women 2.0 (with six years of Women

2.0 on the side on nights and weekends). I realized that I didn't want to be a writer full time, and that's what I had become. I was getting press passes, covering news, and making news. But success as a writer didn't thrill me, and entrepreneurship success is hard to measure. Did we move the needle for women in entrepreneurship? Women 2.0 is definitely the brand I crafted from scratch to attract and inspire the leading women in technology, entrepreneurship, and business. But how do we measure success? Is success an IPO or a billion-dollar valuation? Do you have to be the founder, the CEO, or the chief of staff of a large company, or can you start a boutique consulting business and be considered a success?

While I was ruminating on these thoughts, Girl Geek Dinners kept chugging along regularly. I was hosting dinners at Palantir, Yahoo, Microsoft, Genentech, and other companies with increasing regularity and popularity. One company that reached out to me to sponsor a dinner was Hackbright Academy, a new education company focused on educating women and helping them transition their careers into software engineering. I was intrigued, so I met with the founder and CEO, and we immediately clicked. We shared a vision for pivoting many women's careers into engineering and met regularly after work to talk about how to achieve our goals. I started as an advisor to Hackbright Academy, and when my seventh work anniversary for Women 2.0 was celebrated on LinkedIn, I started feeling the seven-year itch.

The Women 2.0 team had grown to the point where I was managing a team of writers, and we also had more people in our events department. I hired writers and editors, inviting them to check in with me if they would like, but I was generally excited to see the new blood infused into Women 2.0. I trust people I hire to do their jobs well. I believe that we should be starfish, who have the ability to regenerate arms, instead of spiders, who are crippled when they lose a leg. A sustainable organization evolves, and I had built a team I was proud of at Women 2.0.

I wanted to change the ratio in engineering, and at Hackbright Academy we provide that opportunity for women. One of the persistent problems women in technology face is the perception that we are less technical. Successful female CTOs share stories of being ignored in important meetings where technical questions were directed at their nontechnical male colleagues. There is a strong possibility that biases like these directly contribute to the lower rate of funding for startup ventures founded by women, because they are not seen as capable or technical enough. I couldn't go into PR and launch campaigns to change the image of women in the media, but I was excited about the chance to create a new opportunity for women to pivot their careers into software engineering in just ten weeks. I wanted to change the ratio in San Francisco quickly, in the way I knew how, and let other people, like Sheryl Sandberg, work on the global image issue.

At Hackbright Academy, we think every day about how to change the gender ratio of women in technology. We do it through our ten-week engineering fellowship, offered quarterly to a select classroom of women in San Francisco. We also have classes at night and on weekends for women who aren't ready to quit their day jobs and become engineers right away—for women to learn to code on their own time and terms.

It's not just about learning to code. Code is just a language. You can learn to code as easily as you can learn to speak Russian or Chinese. In fact, I jokingly call coding "the new Chinese." A few years ago, wealthy parents would send their children to Chinese school so they could get an edge in life, but today, parents may enroll their children (unfortunately, unconscious bias has them enrolling only their young boys, not girls) in computer camps like iD Tech and Technovation.

This is about changing unconscious bias. This is about creating a world where we recognize that a boardroom or VC office or startup founders' den should be 50/50 male/female. This is about recognizing that this is not the case and that since the population is 50/50, we are missing out on innovation and business opportunities by continuing to uphold the status quo. Diverse teams have been proven time and again to bring better business results, in terms of time, project management, and ROI.

You become more diverse by pursuing all of your interests. You can try things on the side; there are so many hours in a day (and ways to fill the hours). There are meetups and volunteer opportunities—these are all occasions to develop skills and leadership potential.

Failure is inevitable—one cannot possibly succeed at everything. If you try thirty things, you are bound to enjoy or excel in at least two! So say yes to opportunities that cross your path, especially those that require you to learn something new.

<START YOUR OWN COMPANY>

There seem to be a lot of women who think that it's difficult to start a business. They think that there is someone out there who will judge whether or not they are ready. In reality there's no one telling you that you can't start a company, and there are, in fact, many reasons to do so. Over the course of your career, you will have a lot of reasons to network and to attend events on behalf of your own ability to get jobs. Technology is splintering ever further, and it's difficult to know what tomorrow's brand-spanking-new technology trend will be. As a result, you should be thinking of your own career as the company that you work for, as opposed to whatever company is currently signing your paychecks. I'll talk about two different kinds of companies that you should be creating. The first is a consulting company that you own personally, and the second is your first startup. Finally, we'll talk about what it's like to run a business and how to succeed personally as well as professionally.

TWO DIFFERENT COMPANY OPTIONS

Starting a Consulting Company

I have a consulting company where I've worked for thirteen years. It's called Red Queen Technologies LLC. I am the sole owner of that company. Part of my job as a tech contractor was to ensure that I had a steady flow of new jobs coming my way. What you may not realize is that attending networking events to get business for your company is a tax-deductible expense. When I attend meetups, I write off the cost of attendance, transportation to the event, and dinner that I buy for intended clients as expenses for my company. In most countries, professional development is a tax-deductible expense. Throughout this book, I have advocated trying new things to see if they work. This case is no exception: you don't need to wait to start your company until after you know it's going to work. Start one now, and find business to direct its way.

So what are the steps to building your own consulting company? In every state in the United States, you can create your own limited liability company (LLC). This is the fastest way to get a business entity that will let you write off expenses related to your career. File with your department of state to get a business license number (also called a business registration number, a tax identification number, or unified business identifier), and then call (don't use the web interface; it's currently a nightmare of poor design and broken links, and you can at least do other stuff while on phone hold) to get an EIN (employer identification number) from the federal government at IRS.gov. It allows you to write off business expenses while limiting some of the overlap between your personal and professional finances. It'll cost about $210 in Washington State for your LLC formation and your local business license. That's all you have to do to be a business owner.

Still, that's just the logistics. The truth is that the reason you're forming your own company is to give yourself the ability to have a job even if no other company will hire you. There are strategies for creating your own tech consulting company, like that of paying worker's compensation and unemployment insurance so that if you are out of work with any vendor or technical agency, you can collect unemployment from your state. You should consult an accountant to help you with this; it's complicated and you should review your state tax liability carefully. Aside from the financial benefits, there is something special about owning your own company and deciding what title you should have that lets you hold your head up a little bit higher when you need to pass a business card to someone who may or may not want to give you work at a networking event. That I can call myself a senior development director and mean it (and get paid to do it long term) is part of the reason why people have hired me as a consultant.

There are a couple of simple logistics to making sure that you can form your own company and leave yourself open to future options. One thing you need to do is find out whether or not the company name you want to file is in use by searching TESS (Trademark Electronic Search System) at the USPTO (United States Patent and Trademark Office) website. If it is, pick a different name. Let's use the imaginary example of Blue Sun Consulting. If Blue Sun Consulting is a name that has been registered already according to the TESS results, find a new name. Get the Facebook, Twitter, LinkedIn, and other relevant social media handles associated with that name. You may or may not use them right away, but at least you'll have them for the future. Make sure to get the dot-com name for your consulting company. Even now, with all of the great new extensions for top-level domains, most people will still unthinkingly type the name of your company followed by ".com" into a URL search bar. Make it easy for them to find you. Also make sure that your dot-com domain name is an easy one to spell. I frequently use a second-grade reading level as a benchmark.

If you haven't the foggiest notion yet how to get clients, all you need to do is think of yourself as a free or low-cost service provider for your friends and family. You'll build your skills by using them to benefit people who are happier to take a lower-quality product simply because it is inexpensive or free. You'll keep attending networking events to look for jobs. It's just that now you're looking for work to be assigned to your company, instead of looking for jobs you could accept at other companies.

I'll give you a single piece of advice on how to handle your finances: get a damn bookkeeper. You will not like the results if you try to save your own receipts and do your own taxes for an LLC. The time you will save by paying $50 to $100 a month for a solid bookkeeper who will keep your company's expenses and books up to date is worth ten times that amount. Save all your receipts and write the expense category on them right as you get the receipt. Then your accountant has much, much less to do at the end of the year. Having a bookkeeper will cost you a great deal less overall than if you had your accountant track down each of your expenditure categories at the end of the year.

Now you know everything (yes, really) you need to know about starting a consulting company that lets you take on clients and write off business expenses.

Starting a Startup

You have a huge idea for a great company that is going to change the world. It's time to start your own tech startup. So let's have a chat about how to create your own tech startup. Remember that statistically your first several startups will fail. My first two tech startups failed. It wasn't until I co-founded Fizzmint that I actually saw success. You might as well get the first couple of failures over with so you can learn some valuable lessons.

One of the most frightening things to deal with as you're beginning your own company is the idea that somewhere, in a garage in Menlo Park, some other genius is working on the same idea you are. The truth is that the chances of you actively competing with someone else are very low, and if you do have some competition, that's actually a very good thing when it comes to market share and finding funding. Part of marketing metrics involves having competition, and investors are actually much more likely to want to bet on a solid team of technical founders who are leading a pack of people in an emerging niche market in tech rather than an idea that is being developed in isolation and may be ahead of its time. Being way ahead of your time is a bad thing in the world of startup finance; you want to be barely ahead of the rest of the people in your field.

There have been reams of volumes written on how to attract and score funding for startups. The thing to remember is to develop your personal network. Meet with people with similar interests, and join user groups for technology you'll be using in your business. This is where to find not only angel investors looking to skim the cream of the technical bourgeoisie but also people who can support your goals.

Do not get so caught up in your idea that you forget to produce. We've all had billion-dollar ideas, but most of us aren't billionaires. It's very common for people beginning a startup for the first time to get bogged down in paperwork, structuring the company, worrying about ownership and equity, and spending a lot of money on legal work—and by this I mean that those are the mistakes I made the first two times around. Worry instead about two things: talking to your users to find out what they want and iterating your working product as rapidly as possible. To repeat: stop worrying about equity and who's going to have what title and intellectual property protection, and worry about user feedback and iterating working product.

When you are putting a team together to found a company, the mix of personalities is very important, as is the level of respect for each other's skills. You need at least one person with deep as well as broad technical capacity (e.g., a solid C++ developer) who is comfortable leading teams. If that person can execute on their technical specs with a team, they'll end up as VP of engineering. If they're also a visionary and an architect, they'll end up as CTO. You also need someone who is comfortable with people, camera-ready, an excellent leader, and steeped in technology. These are the minimum two people needed to begin a startup. You cannot start a company on your own. Rather, you can start a company on your own, but your likelihood of success is profoundly lower than if you have someone to whom you will be accountable. Please learn from my mistakes there; I tried being a sole founder and crashed hard from lack of support.

Setting goals and achieving them is only satisfactory and realistic when you have someone to share them with on a professional level. Think of the people with whom you will be starting your company as your spouses; there are many commonalities in marriage and startup partners. You will see the worst of each other as well as the best—and you'll see much more of them than your life partners for quite a while. You are working toward a common goal, and sometimes you cannot be at your best; you must have someone to rely on who can challenge and motivate you as well as pick up the slack when you are sick or unavailable. Do not start a company with your best friend. Start a company with someone who you think works as hard or harder than you, whose skills complement yours, and who has excellent communication habits.

Business and the hard work that comes with a startup can leech your creativity. It can drain you, exhaust you, depress you, and fill you with a sense of futility. Having solid partners helps to lift that burden, but part of the way to fix this is to divide the work well. If you have a two-person startup, it is very easy to shove all the technical work onto the CTO and all the administrative work onto the CEO. Do not fall into that trap; you are beginning a company because you strongly believe in your product and your potential. Make sure the CTO can sell the product and the CEO can code. Though one of you will be better than the other at certain tasks, that does not mean you should specialize to the extent of an incapacity to do most of the other person's job. Your skill set must be complementary, not mutually exclusive. In addition, borrow from a twelve-step program, and make a fearless and searching inventory of yourself. Are you the kind of person to whom other people would want to tie their future and their financial security? If you cannot answer in the affirmative, consider taking some time to work on yourself, your abilities, your sense of responsibility, and your ability to resolve conflicts before jumping into the high-pressure startup world.

It's more intimate, in many ways, to have a co-founder of a startup than a spouse. Your co-founder will know more about you than almost anyone else in your life. In fact, your co-founder will know things about you that your friends and spouse don't even know. You can and should feel the need to keep some things hidden from your friends when they're inconvenient or uncomfortable. Fortunately or unfortunately, your co-founder will need to know intimate details about your life, your health, your relationship, what side of the airplane you like to sit on, and how you chew your food.

Co-founders will not judge you about the state of your relationship, but they may know much more about it than your close friends do. You may have friends who are a little bit flaky, but your co-founder never will be. On days when you can't handle something, your co-founder tells you, "It's handled," and you believe her. You will have more close interpersonal time with this person than with possibly anyone else in your life for several years. You'll know this person's credit score and food allergies, and you'll know which one of you should pack the good snacks in your backpack on long plane flights and which one of you will handle the ticketing and hotel accommodations.

You will be in close proximity to this person for hours and days at a time. It's OK to hide your stress and frustration and mental health issues from your friends. After all, you're trying to make sure that you still have friends tomorrow. However, you cannot ever lie to or conceal anything from your co-founder about your mental or physical health. Your co-founder will know everything about you.

This person will know embarrassing things about you, your personal issues with your parents, and the inside of your relationships. After all, you and your co-founder should compensate for each other's weaknesses. You'll have sorted out very quickly which one of you is introverted and which one is extroverted. Possibly you both are one or the other. There cannot be any jealousy between you. After a while, your skill sets will start to diverge from one another. After all, it's likely that you began by having very similar skill sets, which is why you decided to found a startup together.

One of you is going to be more famous than the other one. One of you is going to have to answer customers' angry phone calls. One of you will spend long and exhausting hours programming. Don't be jealous of either party; accept your roles in advance.

If you have competing—as opposed to complementary—goals for the level of publicity and the amount of technical skill that you each wish to acquire over the course of the next several years, you probably shouldn't be founding a startup with this person.

You have my permission to whine about the pressures of your position in the startup. You never have my permission to complain about the level of effort that the other person is putting into your startup. The key things that I looked for in my startup co-founder were a strong work ethic, discretion, and a complementary skill set. Liz is the only person I've ever met who I genuinely believe works harder than I do, and she feels the same about me.

I say, sometimes, that Liz is not my friend. In many ways, she is much more than that. I have a much closer relationship with Liz than I do with almost any other person on earth. She and I know a great deal about each other—like our psychological makeup, our families, and what we can and cannot tolerate on a daily basis.

My friends cannot tell me to get off the Internet. My friends cannot tell me to go home for the day because I'm done. My friends cannot tell me that I need a vacation, because I won't believe them. I believe and do each of these things when Liz tells me to.

Have the deepest respect for the person you're founding your company with, because as I've already mentioned, you are the average of the five people you spend the most time with. Now imagine that your co-founder is three out of the five.

And Liz? It's your turn to pick up the tacos.

WHAT IT'S LIKE RUNNING A BUSINESS

Work-Life Balance and Control

Maintaining a solid work-life balance is crucial—it is the difference between success and burnt-out failure. Do not schedule your work. Schedule your free time and activities. Do not touch work during your free time. Startups are fantastical beasts that eat your free time, your life, your relationships, and your emotional energy. You must recharge to be successful and have the capacity to push forward to each milestone. It is very common to let hobbies and interests die as you are moving in the bootstrapping phase for a startup. Schedule and maintain at least one mental hobby and at least one physical hobby. Your physical and mental well-being are the fuel that lets you pursue your dreams; maintain them diligently. If you play rugby or run or dance or practice yoga, do not stop, no matter how much you believe your company will benefit from a few more hours of your time each week. If you play chess or role-playing games, or are in a book club, do not cease to play or leave the club. You need mental recharging just as much as physical recharging, but people often believe that the tough problems they face as an entrepreneur are enough of a mental challenge for the long week ahead. This is a terrible mistake; your dreams about and joy in creating new projects and products do not drag down your goals—they fuel and supercharge them.

There is a solid reason for my focus on startups as ideal businesses for women to start. People who need flexibility along with achievement need more control over their lives. You do not get total control over your life by taking orders from someone else. Arguably, only the top hundred or so employees in any large organization ever really have control over their lives and schedules and careers, and you should try being one of them at some point in your career. Tech is flexible and full of smart, creative people. It is also high pressure, stressful, deadline ridden, and icily competitive. You should own your piece of the tech world to insulate yourself from the problems that come with having a dozen bosses up the chain to the CEO. More than that, startups are the only real way for a woman to get power in tech, at least right now. There are a few notable exceptions, such as Marissa Mayer and Sheryl Sandberg—or so you might think. In actuality, those two women have the power and positions they have because Mayer was the twentieth employee at Google and Sandberg joined Google in 2001 as a very early employee. The common thread was that they joined intelligent startups very early on and reaped the benefits from it. Go thou and do likewise.

Let us be honest; part of the reason Sandberg and Mayer are so powerful now is the money they made. We all have dreams of cashing out, and the startup world is the best way to do it. No one ever gets rich (in the Western world's definition of that word) working as a corporate drone. You can have a very successful and secure life as a corporate worker, but you will never be independently wealthy, and even if you do get to retire, you will not be able to do so young enough to pursue your real dreams. Have the audacity to become someone you would have admired at the age of ten.

Creating Connections

An excellent reason to be involved in startups is to create connections for yourself. Knowing the people in the area who are focused on creating new products and making companies work is a profoundly valuable asset. Notice that it's an asset, not a fortuitous circumstance. Building your connections and your network takes time and work, but a good startup community is like fizzy soda; it bubbles with talent and energy, and you should drink it in. Send a thank-you card when someone does something nice for you. Work to push other people's interests, and take advantage when you have the connections to trickle down some of the network power you have to the people you will be mentoring. Networking is not just lateral; it is vertical. You will network with senior business people and college students, with recruiters and with executives, and with your own colleagues. Providing your network connections to people newer to the scene does not just make you a good person—it also means that you are helping to build the next crop of talented tech entrepreneurs who will come to you when you have the ability to invest in them.

Finally, talented entrepreneurs can expect rather a lot of something quite startling: fame. You may not have expected it when you got into the field of technical startups, but part of being successful in business is having people call you up to interview you, write about you on their blogs, and tweet to you to request your attention. Depending on how extensive your success is, you may be the subject of print and television interviews and biographical pieces, and at the top end, you may be asked to join charitable endeavors and corporate boards. It may be disorienting at first to field requests from journalists who want to know about your life, but do remember to be kind, polite, and honest, even if you are not entirely open. Remember that your life will be a glass house. Part of the price of your fame will be that you will no longer be able to make negative comments on Facebook and have it blow over. People who are not used to thinking of themselves as thought leaders or public figures can sometimes err on the side of being overly familiar with the public without realizing that their words can truly harm others. A good idea would be to train yourself not to tweet or post to Facebook without taking a ten-second count and rereading your post before hitting "Send" to ensure that nothing there could be interpreted as negative, personally hurtful, libelous, or overly revealing. There is a price to success, and constant criticism from others is that price. Accept that dealing with the price of fame is the ultimate high-class problem, and do your best to be gracious and helpful to the people who helped you and supported you along the way.

<A FINAL NOTE>

I started writing this book thinking that I could dispassionately analyze the women in tech problem from my oh-so-scientific perspective and solve it with the force of my spectacular, world-shattering intellect. I've ended up instead having to be extremely vulnerable with you all. Around every corner lurked personal stories I needed to tell that have brought up frightening or un-dealt-with things from my life, embarrassed me, or shown that I failed. I don't like it. Still, dealing with unprocessed failure is good for you, like fish oil and biking uphill. The constant journey of learning what makes you tick and how you can create a wonderful life for yourself will likewise be difficult, but this journey is one worth making.

I've preached all the way through this book about how the best way to learn anything is to teach it, and now I'm realizing that I learned much more about myself than about the women in tech problem. It's difficult to practice the kind of compassion and empathy necessary to acknowledge the hurtful effects of unconscious social bias without hating others. You'll spend the rest of your life trying to practice it.

There is a common thread running through all our stories: we loved to play games and build things and dream. Over these pages there have been quite a few mentions of Dungeons & Dragons, Legos, the movies *Hackers* and *Sneakers*, and Star Trek. It's difficult to get a quantitative measure of how many young women these stories inspired, but there's no doubt in my mind that they matter hugely to us. Negative and stupid portrayals of women as the hero's girlfriend or decoration hurt us not just out in the open where we talk about it but also on the inside—and the positive stories affect us just as deeply. I've heard more than one woman say, "What would Kathryn Janeway do?" when she didn't know her next move. I've said it myself. If you help create these stories or are a giant fan, please work hard to keep girls and women included in them. When there are no numbers and statistics proving that we can achieve our dreams, sometimes we have to take a leap of faith. These games, characters, tools, and stories can be that last bit of fuel and inspiration we need to reach our goals.

We've tried as hard as possible to stay positive and tell the stories that will help others understand how much technology means to us, but before I close this book, I would like to pay tribute to the astounding bravery of my co-authors. While writing this book, I've requested legal and financial advice about what to do if one of my authors died due to her advocacy—and the fact that this didn't seem unreasonable to me is completely horrifying. Transwomen, women of color, queer people, and advocates for diversity risk being murdered just for being who they are. This is not to mention the bravery of those who might *only* irreparably damage their careers, relationships, and livelihoods by speaking out. Without my extraordinary co-authors, this book would not have happened, and I'm honored that they trusted me to ship this product.

I started out seeing only the injustices in technology, and I wanted to rage and scream and fight. The closer I got to the forest, the more I saw the trees, though. I love the people I know in tech, even though they, I, you, and everyone else make all these social problems just as much as we create the technical solutions. I started realizing that for all my quantitative and computational background, the things that had touched me the most and changed my life the most were stories. Please think for a while about your story and the stories that others have told you. Then, if you're ready, tell someone else. I'd certainly like to hear it.

You'll spend the rest of your life realizing how artful, creative, inspiring, and beautiful technology is as well. If I can give you any single piece of advice, it's this: find your family. Your crew and mentors and colleagues and friends who accompany you throughout your professional life will become your best allies, your source of true criticism, and your underlying support.

Come find us. You're not alone.

<BONUS CHAPTER FOR MEN>

How to Be an Ally and How to Help

I never had a problem with Mitt Romney's use of the phrase "binders full of women." Remember that awkward 2012 statement about his proposed cabinet's lack of women? He said, "I had the chance to pull together a cabinet, and all the applicants seemed to be men. . . . I went to a number of women's groups and said, 'Can you help us find folks?' and they brought us whole binders full of women." Romney realized that he was seeing no women candidates for his cabinet and reached out to people he thought could help him. Instead of congratulating him for his realization and his attempt to (awkwardly) rectify the situation, we crucified him for not already having a network of accomplished women. I think that's a horribly shortsighted way to treat men who want to learn how to help women succeed in tech and business. It's important to be able to make mistakes as you're learning, and I want to help. I have a few suggestions for you, and I'm glad you're listening.

START THE BALL ROLLING

First, as a man who is delivering a product, you can drastically improve your bottom line and reputation by not excluding 51 percent of the population. There are often extremely erroneous assumptions made about how and even whether women will consume a product that is typically made for and marketed to men. Violent video games are the best example. In reasonably smaller numbers, women play the same kinds of games as men but are often completely excluded from marketing campaigns or, worse, are used to sexually decorate those same campaigns. I was so tired of seeing half-naked female Twi'Lek dancers as writhing decorations in Star Wars: The Old Republic that I stopped playing what was otherwise a really fun game. (See Anita Sarkeesian's Tropes Vs. Women in Video Games YouTube series to learn more about this phenomenon of decoration.) If turnabout were fair play, the situation would not be so dire, but advertising for traditionally female-oriented games typically does not include naked men serving cosmopolitans to lounging femmes. You can improve your profit margin by bringing even one female voice into a technical marketing campaign. It can open up consumer access to your product and thereby increase your accomplishments as a producer. Even better, bringing a female designer and developer into the project can build in some advocacy for a broader market. The most violent, bro-tastic games still have a small female market, and adding even one well-rounded female character (well-rounded in terms of *story*, y'all) to the lineup of player characters can double, triple, or exponentially expand your female demographic.

WOMEN ARE NOT DECOR

You can also positively affect your company's promotional efforts toward women as product consumers. Stories abound of "beer girls" being used to promote technical events like hackathons. Photos of skimpily clad women serving steins to nerds feverishly coding then appear on social media, and if you are seen in one of those pictures, you will become less desirable in the job market. If you encounter a promotional event that uses women as decor in any way, have a chat with whoever is planning the event and suggest changes to prevent your company becoming a byword for idiocy regarding gender relations. I was just at an industry party for a company where the entertainment was—I absolutely kid you not—two exotic dancers on poles. Having experienced the fun of being at the center of a screaming Internet tantrum before, I chose not to Instagram the situation. I thought an iron fist in a velvet glove would solve the problem better, and I had a quiet word with one of the biggest partners of that company. I mentioned that perhaps in the future, the offending company would want to ask themselves where I and the other female entrepreneurs would be taking our business and who would want to be associated with a company that made such poor decisions. As far as I know, it worked and will not happen again—at that company. If all else fails, do not go to the event, and make your reasoning known to your supervisor. Saying that you don't want to end up explaining yourself on Facebook the next day is a funny and honest way of handling the situation.

WATCH OUT FOR THAT
UNCONSCIOUS BIAS

The second way men are encountering the integration of women into technology is in the acquisition of female hires. Men are starting to feel pressure in every area of technology to evaluate and hire women if possible. However, no one is teaching them how to evaluate women in comparison to men. Men and women frequently publicly exhibit different kinds of ambition, and understanding what traits will benefit your team can help you both add gender diversity to your workplace and make for more comfortable conversations with your HR department when it comes to the percentage of women you hire.

Understand something: no one believes that women are deliberately being left out of technology or that there is some vast conspiracy to prevent women from getting the kind of prestigious and lucrative jobs that men enjoy in tech. Men are almost never consciously trying to keep women out of tech. They have been unconsciously socialized into hiring people who fit their unexamined assumptions about what makes "outspoken leaders," "aggressive individualists," "geek culture lovers," and "lone wolf geniuses."

Does this situation sound familiar? A VP of diversity is drilling a hiring manager about interviews and asking, "Jane had the same years of experience and leadership as Joe and a longer work history; what made you go with Joe over Jane, even though we're working to get more women into the company?" The hiring manager responds, "Jane's résumé looked the same, but when we explored her experience, she was much more hesitant when answering questions and seemed like she didn't have the confidence to handle this kind of high-pressure, eff-it-ship-it environment. Plus she had a longer work history because she has repeated gaps where she's dropped out of her job unexpectedly; I can't see her as a reliable and potentially successful hire."

How can you blame the hiring manager for making that decision? How could anyone? That is what I mean when I say men are not excluding women. Until a good work history has been redefined as one in which gaps for caretaking are seen as evidence of reliable and admirable commitment to family and nonnegative, it unfortunately falls to women to learn to project the confidence and communication that will make tech hiring managers believe that they'll be good hires. It's now also the serious responsibility of men to start learning how to look past the kinds of cultural biases that penalize women's typical life trajectories. Some of this does rest with the companies themselves; working to make telecommuting and flexibility part of the package means that they can retain good female hires in a way they have not previously been able to accomplish. This means that the dreaded "she'll just get pregnant and all our financial and educational investment in her will leave with her" conundrum doesn't come up. In addition, male managers need help interpreting the responses they're given in order to respect caregiver choices rather than penalize them.

Here are some helpful facts as you learn and teach: half of all American women will not have children, and anecdotally at least, that population is overrepresented in tech. In addition, the majority of millennial men expect to share parenting and care duties at least equally, meaning that there's no way anymore to tell by sight or gender which of your incoming hires will expect a great deal of parental leave. A thoughtful and farseeing manager would create egalitarian policies now to deal with the influx of men expecting extended parental leave.

BE DELIBERATE

If you are part of the hiring process in your company, ask yourself whether all the qualified internal female candidates know about openings. You can be the person who is the conduit of information to women in your company about job openings and can provide the information that all your female colleagues and employees need in order to try for better positions. Often just the fact that you suggested the opening to a female colleague or employee can let her know that she is qualified for the position. Women do not typically negotiate or push for advancement if they do not know that negotiation is acceptable and pushing is required to get ahead, as we've discussed in the salary negotiations portion of the book. Providing women with that sort of information about the corporate culture in which you are embedded can create a lifelong member of your professional network and a better place to work. The gender gap in pay almost completely disappears when the words "salary negotiable" appears in job notices; otherwise women will assume that the salary is set when the position is advertised. Men will negotiate regardless of that announcement, so telling women that the salary is negotiable will improve their lot without decreasing the negotiating ability or expectations of men applying for the same position.

OMG PREGNANCY OMG

Here is how to handle parental leave when one of your employees comes to you and announces that she is pregnant. Rule 1: Do exactly as Miss Manners instructs: say "Congratulations!" and absolutely nothing else until she's done talking. Rule 2: If she pauses for feedback, say "I'm here to listen." This opens the conversation up so that she can let you know if there are any concerns about her pregnancy;

she may be ill, anticipating a difficult pregnancy, or not wish for the news to be openly discussed in the office yet. Rule 3: Do not ask her how much time she will be missing from work or when she wants to leave her job. You will almost certainly need to talk to your HR department to find out your company's policy on maternity leave and holding the position open for her return. Rule 4: Stop. Talking. Seriously. Right at that moment, it is completely normal to be worrying about your projects and deliverables, and to be thinking in terms of the impact that this woman's pregnancy will have on your bottom line. You would not be a good boss if you were not examining all the angles, but you risk serious legal and internal issues if you verbally cast a major life event for this woman in terms of your project deadlines. Also, that's a bit of a jackass move if you say it out loud. Follow up the next day after asking HR to help you draft any emails or communications from you to her in order to minimize this risk.

You can handle a woman's return to work after maternity leave by never dropping your standards. That may seem like odd advice, coming from people who advocate for women's acceptance and promotion in technology, but you do neither yourself nor the women with whom you work any favors by accepting low-quality work from a woman who is experiencing pressures from family life. Drop the amount of work but never lower your expectations of the quality. New parents will often feel the need to return to work rapidly in order to preserve their job or career track, and sometimes it is up to you as the supervisor to start slowly with the amount of work assigned to the woman. It is very common for the woman to return and instantly take up where she left off but be unable to complete tasks at first. She may be ill, is 100 percent guaranteed to be sleep deprived, may have had a hard birth, and may need some understanding on the quantity of work she can accomplish at first. This period does not last for long, but burning her out in the first two weeks and demanding the same quantity while still expecting quality would be poor thanks for her contribution to the continuation of the human species.

Women are team members just like everyone else. All people are different; treat them all differently—but equally. The understanding that a woman needs during the hiring process or during maternity leave is different from but equal to the concern that a chronically ill male colleague requires. As long as you are spending the same amount of mental and social energy handling your employees, worry less about difference and more about equality.

LEADING PEOPLE WHO DON'T LOOK LIKE YOU

No one trains managers in empathy. We train new managers to use project management software, to interface with clients, and to fill out time sheets, but being a manager means caring about your people. When is the last time you, as a manager, faced training that taught you that you have profound power over the lives of the people who work for you and that your thoughtlessness is deeply cruel when you force people to operate in an environment that harms them?

I'm using strong language because over the last fifteen-odd years, I've seen an unbelievable amount of mindless callousness toward people who deviate from the norm. Much of what I've seen involves treating people with disabilities or medical conditions as inconveniences gladly shed when the workday is through—and absolutely ensuring that people with disabilities cannot attend the after-work and networking events that are so vital to a successful career. Many managers don't realize how much harder it is to get a job when you're differently abled, transgender, female, older, or any of the other categories that aren't single, white, young, straight, and male.

Your job as a manager is very different than the one you did while on the team. As a manager, your job is to help your team succeed.

One of the biggest issues I see new managers struggling with is the idea that the team is theirs. Their responsibility, their charge, their trust. They've been entrusted with people who have less voice than they do about the conditions under which they work, the conflict they experience, and the situations they find themselves in. The worst managers I've seen aren't the ones who deliberately push people around. The worst managers are the ones who assume a peer relationship with their team and take absolutely no responsibility for the success and comfort of the people they've been charged with protecting and promoting. "It's not my fault; I didn't know that poster would make her uncomfortable, and if it did, why didn't she tell me?" Don't blame your employees for not doing your job for you.

Managers often think to themselves, *If someone has a problem with these arrangements, I'll hear about it. They'll just speak up.* Wrong. If you're in a position of power over people's lives and ability to put food on the table, you'll never hear about a problem with the hotel accommodations, the food selection, the air-conditioning, the pet allergies, the disability access, the racist posters in the ladies' bathrooms, or the pressure to consume too much alcohol.

Your leadership is especially important when your team is traveling somewhere. When people are moved outside their comfort zone, they have needs that they expect you to be thinking about and to handle. If you have a team member who is disabled and you plan an after-party at a rooftop bar with no elevator, you won't hear from that person about your poor choice to create an "optional" event that your workers are expected to attend for job and networking reasons. Instead, that disabled person will simply say "I'm not up to it tonight" and head back to the hotel. How are they supposed to speak up? They have no power, you pay their bills, and if they complain, they're a party killer instead of a friend and colleague.

This is not an analogy; it's happened to me—I've been the one who chose not to say anything because I didn't want to be the bitch who killed the party. It's your job to put yourself in the position of each person on the team and to ask yourself if they'll all be comfortable and able to succeed in the environment you're forcing them to operate in.

Yes, you're forcing them to do what you want. If you're the person who decides if employees stay or go, you literally have the power to turn off their electricity, pull their kids out of school, have their car repossessed, or cause them emotional and social pain and shame. Do you think that people are going to just speak up when they're uncomfortable? Or are they going to keep their mouth shut, start looking for another job, and bad-mouth the poor management you're providing? Take a look at recent news stories about the working conditions at large tech companies to see what happens when people finally start talking about how poorly they were treated.

I've seen a lot of instances of poor management, especially when traveling for work. I've seen blind people unable to attend work parties because dogs weren't allowed inside. I've seen people with severe animal allergies expected to work in small offices with service animals. I've seen a single step down into a restaurant prevent two people in wheelchairs from attending a party that would have been their only shot to spend time with the CEO.

Hear what people aren't saying.

Here's a good example: Say you're a project manager. Your dev manager decides to send you to the big yearly conference for your area of tech. You book the rooms for your team, set up the reservations for dinner on two nights, and book eight seats on flights. Then the email from your team member who has a mobility disorder arrives. "Can I talk to the airline myself? I want to do an upgrade to first class." You're only human, and the rage beast in the back of your head snarls, "Dammit! I've been trying to get them to socialize with the team, and now they have to wreck it by moving to first class again!"

I've seen managers respond angrily to requests to have travel arrangements changed because they're seeing that request through the eyes of someone working on team solidarity—or they're simply cutting costs. Unfortunately, the state of air travel can be horrible and will certainly be more expensive for people with disabilities. Often the fastest way to handle discomfort and ensure that there will be someone to help them is to do an airline upgrade. It may seem classless for them not to sit with the team (pun intended), but it can be a shortcut to take care of their own needs without troubling their manager. When you know that a member of your team has a disability, you may think that you know what's best for that person. Being visibly physically disabled absolutely means that people treat you as if you're mentally or socially disabled as well. Don't think you know better than someone who's been managing a disability for years. Let people make their own choices, and find a different way to accomplish your goals.

Or how about this one: You're a new manager. You want to invite your team out to pizza and beer and make it a regular thing. In a fairly common circumstance, you have five white men, one East Asian man, and one South Asian woman working for you. After three Friday happy hours, the woman has never come, the East Asian man came to the first one and not any of the following ones, and the five white men are regulars. Why do you think this is? Have you noticed that it's happening?

To realize what is going on here, look at the socioeconomic factors on your team. I won't say that it's always the case, but for many women in the United States and around the world, a job with clearly defined working hours is a blessing that lets them support a family and still spend time with them. I'm not just talking about children; there are many cultures that place emphasis on care for the aged, and given my experience managing, it's generally women who bear the burden of that care. Let's not pretend that after-hours socializing is totally unrelated to career success. If you don't know that woman as well as you know the men who do attend happy hour, you're less likely to promote her. Instead, think about how to make team socializing happen on the job. Can you do a team lunch potluck on Fridays? A potluck always helps, since people can be guaranteed that there will be something they can eat. Can you do a family-friendly picnic as an off-site meeting some Monday or Saturday? There are better options than the unspoken requirement that even if you're not getting paid for it, your tired ass shows up for happy hour or you don't get promoted. That invisible power structure is a major barrier to the success of women and minorities of all kinds, and you can help open it up.

The East Asian man on your team may be lactose intolerant (a common genetic difference) and unwilling to insult your whole team by admitting that pizza makes him ill. This is serious—who would want to tell their friends and colleagues that they don't like their food? Ever thought about rotating the location of your happy hour to include lots of different experiences and restaurants? Not only does sharing new experiences make for a better team—it offers choices for people who may not want to tell you that your plan doesn't work for them.

There are lots of reasons your team might be different at happy hour. Don't pretend that it's not your problem when your not-so-subtle power over your team is what creates burdens for people who don't look like you.

Seeing situations through your team members' eyes can help you avoid being unthinkingly exclusive. If they make a request that seems odd, don't immediately deny it. Ask yourself why they might be making the request to begin with. If the women on your team never show up for happy hour, ask yourself what about the environment could make a woman uncomfortable. Not going to Hooters is an obvious choice, but a more subtle one might be to ensure that the social situation doesn't change to one that is more sexually charged when the rest of your team gets tipsy.

It's your responsibility to take care of your people. You have power, and whether intentionally or not, you're using it. If you want to ask me questions in private, send me an email. I'll always confidentially help if I can. I won't blame you, I will never shame you publicly for asking for help, and I'll help you find mentors and training to really make your workplace better. I think it's a damned shame the way we publicly pillory men who ask for help on diversity issues, and I'll never do that to you if you're really trying to help and grow. I do wish you the best of luck, and I know you can help make the lives of others better.

<ACKNOWLEDGMENTS>

This book is the creation of the entire tech community, and while I tried to remember everyone who provided help, so many people threw their effort behind this that I will certainly leave some out. I apologize in advance and thank you so very, very much for all you've done.

This book began with Kickstarter, and when I was putting the campaign together, I spent two rum-fueled hours having a video-chat session with the amazing Dan Shapiro, creator of Robot Turtles, CEO of Glowforge, and Searrle tech startup *impresario* extraordinaire. Dan gave me wonderful advice on how to create the proper economic incentives for my largest Kickstarter yet, and his instructions have saved me a world of hurt. Dan, by presenting a copy of this book to me at any time, you will receive one beer and one bowl of noodles. Margot Atwell, our community manager throughout the Kickstarter process, helped make sure I didn't screw anything up too badly and fixed a last-minute mistake that could have been horrible.

A gigantic thanks goes to the biggest supporters of the book on Kickstarter. Without the phenomenal personal and financial support of Dan Dunham, Sean Hastings, Michelle Sandford, Meg Layton, Genevieve Bell, Khalil "Pilgrim" Sehnaoui, Rebecca Norlander, Laura Miller, Elle Plato, Tamzen Cannoy, and Jon Callas, this book would be nowhere. I am deeply grateful for your trust and kindness. I hope you'll enjoy the book you helped bring about!

The Seattle tech community has been wonderful and supportive. Brett Eddy provided excellent advice on the self-publishing and printing route, and it saved me some serious trouble. Paul Watts inspires me to be kind and provided networking and assistance in the community. Fortunato Vega's warmth and generosity with his network and people skills is unparalleled. Chris "Darth Vlogger" Pirillo helped hugely with the Kickstarter video production in terms of advice, technical support, and equipment recommendations. Ali Mohsenian and the Arc Media Studios crew did a spectacular and highly discounted editing job on the Kickstarter video, which turned out beautifully. Daniel Mimura's shooting of the video was as artistic and perfectly lit as everything else he does. Dan Savage is a tech entrepreneur and sales guru par excellence, and his friendship and advocacy as well as his insistent advertising on my behalf are a huge part of why the Kickstarter campaign succeeded. Brett Greene, Rebecca Lovell, Joshua "Red" Russak, Gina Phillips, Sherry Zins Calvert, Diane Najm, Seaton Gras, Ken Carlson, Robin Held, Erica Melzer, Adam Philipp, Seth Talbott, Amber Osborne, Greg Bulmash, Holly Saultman, Bob Crimmins, Elise Worthy, Gary Ritner, Mary Jesse, Jonathan Sposato, Susie Lee, Jeff Reifman, Caitlin Goetze, Brandy Rhodes, and all the 601 Club members have been unbelievably supportive and kind. Lisa Weeks especially has been a friend, ally, and inspiration for me on how to stay kind and compassionate and not beat the crap out of people even when they are clearly asking for it—as well as just being totally f***ing awesome. Don Sheu and Tammy Lee are stellar members of the Puget Sound Python community and have been noisy in their encouragement and support. Heather Redman provided mentorship and sharp questions. Janis Machala and the Emerging Growth Women's Roundtable group have been a priceless resource. Lisa Sandoval from the Seattle Colleges system has been a quiet and strong voice for years, working to increase diversity and achievement in Seattle, and she's an inspiration. Shannon Anderson and Jason Carl helped in innumerable ways in my career and my life. Erica McGillivray and Susie Rantz at GeekGirlCon provided a wonderful platform for our message. Georgene Jones kept the books on the straight and narrow.

In New York, Andy Dirnberger provided humor and last-minute Python fixes, and made me laugh. Elissa Shevinsky listened to me wail on the phone about how haaaarrrrrd writing a book is, and then kicked my ass into gear. She's truly a #LadyBoss. Jesse Noller, Portia Burton, Kenneth Love, and Nick Coghlan, members-at-large of the Python community, provided great feedback and access to a wonderful world of acceptance and tech. Thanks so much to Erin Jacobs for contributing wonderful advice.

Jim Burrows was a wonderful ear and supported me through some hard conversations that helped me be more comfortable sharing some of my history. Mike and Dr. Mary Beth Janke taught me some very important lessons about being a leader during the writing of this book, which have hopefully filtered through. I'm grateful to Holly Gray, Kim Obbink, John Kaminski, and the sadly missed Robert Vunder for advice. Jason Lewis is my honored intellectual opponent on many subjects in diversity. He has proved to me that civil discourse on the Internet is possible—nay, enjoyable. Long may he disagree with me! Louis Kowolowski stepped up with the tech support—not that I ever, like, *really* needed it. I have shamelessly cribbed G. Clifford Williams's thoughtful points about the minority experience in tech.

Several people I've never met in real life but who provided deep insight, advice, connections, or inspiration during the Kickstarter campaign are Ellen Feaheny, Anar Simpson, and Vivek Wadhwa; I'm grateful for the energy and time you spent, and I hope you enjoy the end product!

Thank you to Kyle Alspach, editor of the *Stories from Women in Tech* blog on Medium. Hundreds of women volunteered to share their stories in this book, and I wanted badly to see all of them out there for everyone to read. Kyle, an internationally respected journalist out of Boston, stepped up and has created a huge hit with Kaya Thomas, his co-editor and a truly spectacular writer.

Thanks to my family: Dad, Mom, Marvin, Melanie, Frannie, Merry, Elisa, and everyone else who put up with a year of "I can't make it this time." Please don't leave me off the invite list to Christmas! I can't put all my thanks into words here, but without you and your love, this would never have been possible.

My friends and colleagues in the infosec community have gone so far beyond any help I could have hoped for that they are practically in orbit. Thank you to Marc Rogers for putting me in touch with Keren Elazari and mutually vouching for us; he was our transitive trust network. Thank you to Brad "Renderman" Haines for listening to me bitch about anything and everything and providing emotional support while I was outlining this damned book. Thanks to Amélie Erin Koran for helping me clarify and rephrase some of my thoughts on transgender rights and for being a swell human. Aiden Riley "Caezar" Eller crosses over from the Seattle tech scene to the infosec world for me, and has been a pillar of mentorship for people who just needed a little extra help to succeed. Thanks to Deviant Ollam for asking a sticky and irritating question at the exact right time, causing me to rewrite my autobiography and make it ten times better. Thanks to William Scannell for much-valued assistance. Thank you to my crew, the Psychoholics: Krux, PunkAB, Fish, Flirzan, Servo, Puking Monkey, Toph, F9, Tangy, Voltage Spike, Greenwalker, Clutch, EvilPacket, Sqrt, and Kermit. Stop being so awesome, or Las Vegas will just be a smoking hole in the ground one of these days. FYP! Thanks to Ada Zebra, the executive director of InfoSec Unlocked, and Tyler Walker, its lead web developer, for running a hell of a program at DEF CON and stepping up to handle parts of the InfoSec Unlocked initiative that I was starting to let slide as I worked on this book. Thanks to the Dream Team of infosec pros who have been participating in the InfoSec Unlocked broadcasts for helping to develop some of the ideas I've used here for cutting through the bull, including Russ "v3rtigo" Rogers, Nikita "Niki7a" Caine Kronenberg, Luna

Lindsey, and Sandy "Mouse" Clark. Finally, thanks to Jeff "The Dark Tangent" Moss for creating DEF CON and giving me the opportunity to meet so many wonderful people.

A huge thank you to Ryan "LostboY" Clarke, the official DEF CON cryptographer, and Mike Selinker, über-gamer and creator of Pathfinder and the Cards against Humanity treasure hunt, for creating amazing Easter egg puzzles for this book and being stellar and inspiring human beings. LosT created the Mystery Challenge that brought me together with my crew at DEF CON, and he's without a doubt one of the smartest people I have ever met. He creates puzzles and challenges every year that completely blow my mind. Mike is a loudmouth about social justice among the nerderati, funny as hell, and a brilliant game designer who works with the stellar Gaby Weidling. I'm honored that they're contributing, and the only thing that irritates me is that I am the single human who isn't allowed to solve the puzzles they're creating for the book! Thanks also to Tero Tilus of SC5 and to a distinguished anonymous contributor who created the Python code for the cover of the book; you're a wonderful human and a true ally.

A special mention goes to my mentors and dear friends Jon Callas and Tamzen Cannoy. They're bloody well family at this point. The level of support and encouragement I've received from Jon and Tamzen goes beyond anything I could have hoped for. Jon was one of my two alpha readers for this book and has been an absolute pillar as I fought through impostor syndrome and various levels of cluelessness and fear. I am not exaggerating in any way when I say that this book would not exist without them. Thanks for the buttons, levers, and wheels—some of which I'm sure I don't even know about.

A shamefully incomplete list of some of the great mentors and teachers I've had in my academic career, and part of the reason I care so much about mentorship now, includes professors Birol Yeşilada, Ronald Tammen, David Kinsella, Robert Axelrod, Rick

Riolo, Scott Page, Kelly Brennan, Brent Northup, and Barry Ferst. Thank you for all those hours making my brain a better place; I'm doing my best to pass on your herculean effort to as many students as I can.

My other alpha reader for the book was Hesper Hobsburhg, and her perfect English and intense attention has been a gift to the clarity of this book. My editor, Hannah Elnan, has been a triumph of support and intelligent questions. The biggest gift Hannah's given me, however, is her trust that when I say something that sounds very strange to her, it will make sense to my nerd people! Thank you, Hannah; it's an honor and a pleasure working with you.

My cat, Frankie Fangs, was the best writing companion possible and the optimal use of a quarter of my desk space. I shall buy him a treat for being a good friend, fuzz-nugget, and purr-face. If there are any strange typos in this book it's because he was walking across the keysojfo9jeosodjfsdfsfdfsfsdff2222 . . .

Thank you to everyone who's ever worked on and helped bring the Star Trek universe to life. It's made a huge difference to me and millions of other women who just needed to see an example they could emulate. PS: My super awesome collection is photos with Star Trek cast members, so if you're a cast member and you see me lurking, I'm not stalking you or being creepy; I'm just trying to take lots of pictures of you and make you understand how much I love you.

My godfather, Michael Gruber, offered hugely valuable publishing advice from his distinguished career as a novelist, scotch, various inappropriate and funny comments, and a wonderful ear. My friend and fellow Shadowrun geek Mike Reinhardt helped clarify the tech interview chapter, acted as a sounding board, and was part of the inspiration for me to write this book in the first place. Rose Jeannette Carter, Sean Prather, and M. Ramon Padilla helped create me as well as this book. Jennifer Stephens Perevodchikov and Toby Eaton Cowell were lovely and supportive friends through this whole agonizing process and fed me huge quantities of chocolate when required. Carly Slater, Rick Sass, and Tamsyn Cunningham of Beacon Workshops have been rock solid in their advice and support. Thank you to Father Michael Ryan and TerryAnn Bowen for moral support and courage.

Liz Dahlstrom, my colleague, erstwhile co-founder, and long-time partner: thank you for your tireless capacity, brilliance, and insight. My whole team at Fizzmint are heroes and geniuses with whom I'm honored to work every day. We're going to change the world together.

To my co-authors, Keren Elazari, Kristin Toth Smith, Kamilah Taylor, Miah Johnson, Brianna Wu, Angie Chang, and Katie Cunningham: I'm unspeakably honored that you trusted me enough to give me your time and effort. We're the ones who made it to the end, and we didn't let the negativity and hatred stop this book from coming out. I've joked a few times about what it's like project managing seven famous women, but the truth is that I could not have hoped for a better, braver, more honest team. I admire you all beyond anything I could express. None of these outstanding women are to blame or are responsible for the content or accuracy of my advice, but they've each inspired me to make this book as worthy of them as I possibly can.

Finally, my husband, Dean. I don't know why I'm thanking you. You did nothing but distract me the entire way through this process with your presents of chocolate, invites to late-night World of Warcraft raids, and jokes. You stopped me from concentrating, made me eat, told me to go outside, and did the dishes very, very loudly while I was trying to write. Clearly, you are a terrible influence on me. In exchange for all that effort on your part, I can only offer you my utter love and possibly make you a pie. But it will be a really, really good pie. Please don't murder me in my sleep if I ever decide to write another book.

<RESOURCES>

BOOTCAMPS

Ada Developers Academy (adadevelopersacademy.org)

Code Fellows (codefellows.org)

Hackbright Academy (hackbrightacademy.com)

BOOKS

Cracking the Coding Interview by Gayle Laakmann McDowell

Lean In: Women, Work, and the Will to Lead by Sheryl Sandberg

Lean Out: The Struggle for Gender Equality in Tech and Start-Up Culture by Elissa Shevinsky

Unfinished Business: Women Men Work Family by Anne-Marie Slaughter

VIDEOS

"How to Shake Hands" by Tarah Wheeler Van Vlack (igniteseattle
.com/2015/05/18/how-to-shake-hands-tarah-wheeler-van-vlack/)

"Your Body Language Shapes Who You Are" by Amy Cuddy (ted
.com/talks/amy_cuddy_your_body_language_shapes_who_you_
are?language=en)

ORGANIZATIONS

Anita Borg Institute (anitaborg.org)

Black Girls Code (blackgirlscode.com)

CODE2040 (code2040.org)

PyLadies (pyladies.com)

Women in Tech Council (witcouncil.org)

<BIBLIOGRAPHY>

INTRODUCTION

http://www.nytimes.com/2008/11/16/business/16digi.html

APPLYING FOR JOBS AND THE TECH RÉSUMÉ

http://www.nytimes.com/2015/07/13/business/rising-economic-insecurity-tied-to-decades-long-trend-in-employment-practices.html
http://www.womansday.com/life/work-money/tips/a6415/never-say-on-a-job-interview/
http://workplace.stackexchange.com/questions/12497/do-i-have-to-put-references-available-upon-request-on-my-resume

THE DEVELOPER

http://www.jamaicaobserver.com/news/Jamaica-has-highest-percentage-of-women-managers-globally---ILO-report

TECH INTERVIEWS

Moss-Racusin, Corinne A., John F. Dovidio, Victoria L. Brescoll, Mark J. Graham, and Jo Handelsman. "Science Faculty's Subtle Gender Biases Favor Male Students." *Proceedings of the National Academy of Sciences of the United States of America* 109, no. 41 (2012): 16474–16479. http://www.pnas.org/content/109/41/16474.full.pdf
http://fortune.com/2014/08/26/performance-review-gender-bias/
http://www.theatlantic.com/features/archive/2014/04/the-confidence-gap/359815/
http://observer.com/2013/02/race-tech-media-silicon-valley-pattern-matching-jamelle-bouie-jason-calacanis/
https://www.washingtonpost.com/news/innovations/wp/2014/02/14/dropboxs-hiring-practices-explain-its-disappointing%E2%80%8B-lack-of-female-employees/
http://www.forbes.com/sites/nickmorgan/2014/06/10/why-do-first-impressions-matter/

Gladwell, Malcolm. *Blink: the Power of Thinking without Thinking.* New York: Back Bay Books, 2005.
http://www.itworld.com/article/2705092/careers/got-a-job-interview--don-t-wear-a-suit.html
http://www.nytimes.com/2011/10/13/fashion/makeup-makes-women-appear-more-competent-study.html
http://www.cnn.com/2007/US/Careers/02/02/cb.tall.people/

TYPES OF TECH JOBS AND SALARY NEGOTIATIONS
http://bits.blogs.nytimes.com/2015/02/28/silicon-valley-shuttle-drivers-vote-to-join-union/
http://www.forbes.com/sites/meghanbiro/2014/01/12/telecommuting-is-the-future-of-work/
http://www.lni.wa.gov/WorkplaceRights/Wages/Overtime/Exemptions/default.asp
http://www.forbes.com/sites/lisaquast/2014/03/31/job-seekers-8-tips-to-negotiate-your-starting-salary/
http://archive.washtech.org/news/industry/display.php?ID_Content=457
http://www.forbes.com/sites/realspin/2012/05/21/mind-the-malefemale-income-gap-but-dont-exaggerate-it/
Schneider, Andrea Kupfer, Catherine H. Tinsley, Sandra I. Cheldelin, and Emily T. Amanatullah. "Likeability v. Competence: The Impossible Choice Faced by Female Politicians, Attenuated by Lawyers." *Duke Journal of Gender Law & Policy* 17, no. 2 (2010); *Marquette Law School Legal Studies Paper* no. 10–42. http://ssrn.com/abstract=1691736
https://hbr.org/2013/04/for-women-leaders-likability-a/
http://stevehanov.ca/blog/index.php?id=67, http://blogs.cornell.edu/info2040/2014/09/28/using-game-theory-for-salary-negotiation/
Lombera, David Carrillo. "Analysis of Two-Party Salary Negotiations: Factors Impeding a Mutually-Beneficial Joint Agreement." Masters diss., 2007. http://bibliotecadigital.fgv.br/dspace/bitstream/handle/10438/3805/acf16b.pdf?sequence=1
Axelrod, Robert. *The Evolution of Cooperation.* New York: Basic Books, Inc., Publishers, 1984.
https://www.washingtonpost.com/posteverything/wp/2015/05/21/the-best-way-to-way-to-eliminate-the-gender-pay-gap-ban-salary-negotiations/
https://hbr.org/2014/06/why-women-dont-negotiate-their-job-offers/

http://career-advice.monster.com/salary-benefits/negotiation-tips/salary-negotiation-gender-wage-gap/article.aspx
http://www.salary.com/why-women-don-t-negotiate/
http://www.npr.org/2015/04/23/401468571/
some-companies-fight-pay-gap-by-eliminating-salary-negotiations
https://www.linkedin.com/
pulse/20130723030236-69244073-do-women-really-civilize-men
http://www.nytimes.com/2013/07/21/opinion/sunday/why-men-need-women.html
http://www.salon.com/2012/04/03/must_women_civilize_men/
http://www.cnn.com/2012/05/07/tech/web/brogrammers/

COMMUNICATION ON THE JOB

http://www.bloomberg.com/news/articles/2015-06-02/
the-best-e-mail-signature-is-actually-the-worst
http://lifehacker.com/5984417/how-i-went-from-1000-emails-to-inbox-zero-and-stayed-there-with-mailstrom
https://www.psychologytoday.com/blog/the-introverts-corner/200911/
introversion-and-the-energy-equation
Cain, Susan. *Quiet: The Power of Introverts in a World That Can't Stop Talking.* New York: Crown, 2012.
Capretz, Luiz Fernando. "Personality Types in Software Engineering." *International Journal of Human-Computer Studies* 58 (2003): 207–214. http://eng.uwo.ca/electrical/faculty/mcisaac_k/docs/mbti-IJHCS-v.pdf
http://gender.stanford.edu/news/2011/
women-leaders-body-language-matters
http://universe.byu.edu/2011/06/26/short-people-face-bias-disadvantages/
http://www.forbes.com/sites/carolkinseygoman/2013/05/22/
why-women-in-business-should-shake-hands/
https://www.youtube.com/watch?v=A36b_GRjvtU
http://www.forbes.com/sites/dailymuse/2012/07/19/
why-your-handshake-matters-and-how-to-get-it-right/
http://www.nytimes.com/2014/09/28/fashion/the-bro-hug-embracing-a-change-in-custom.html

THE FAMILY

http://www.pewsocialtrends.org/2013/03/14/modern-parenthood-roles-of-moms-and-dads-converge-as-they-balance-work-and-family/

http://www.businessmanagementdaily.com/glp/11664/Maternity-Leave-Laws.html

Brush, Candida G., Patricia G. Greene, Lakshmi Balachandra, and Amy E. Davis. "Women Entrepreneurs 2014: Bridging the Gender Gap in Venture Capital." *Diana Report* (2014). http://www.babson.edu/Academics/centers/blank-center/global-research/diana/Documents/diana-project-executive-summary-2014.pdf

http://www.nytimes.com/2008/06/15/magazine/15parenting-t.html

Hochschild, Arlie, and Anne Machung. *Second Shift*. New York: Penguin Books, 2003.

Van Gorp, Kayla. "The Second Shift: Why it is Diminishing but Still an Issue." *Undergraduate Review: a Journal of Undergraduate Student Research* 14 (2013): 31–37. http://fisherpub.sjfc.edu/cgi/viewcontent.cgi?article=1100&context=ur

Kelly, Maura, and Elizabeth Hauck. "Doing Housework, Redoing Gender: Queer Couples Negotiate the Household Division of Labor." *Journal of GLBT Family Studies* 11, no. 5 (2015): 438–464. http://www.tandfonline.com/doi/pdf/10.1080/1550428X.2015.1006750

PERSONAL BRANDING

http://geekfeminism.wikia.com/wiki/Who_is_harmed_by_a_%22Real_Names%22_policy%3F

http://hiring.monster.com/hr/hr-best-practices/recruiting-hiring-advice/attracting-job-candidates/diversity-tech-hiring.aspx

http://www.usatoday.com/story/money/2013/11/14/make-your-next-performance-review-your-best/3525155/

MENTORSHIP

http://money.usnews.com/money/blogs/outside-voices-careers/2010/01/13/13-tips-on-finding-a-mentor

http://www.businessinsider.com/why-teaching-helps-you-learn-2013-7

http://www.businessnewsdaily.com/7864-mentoring-career-benefits.html

http://www.huffingtonpost.com/julie-kantor/stem-mentoring-im-in-now-_1_b_5503609.html

https://hbr.org/2010/09/why-men-still-get-more-promotions-than-women

http://www.nytimes.com/2013/04/14/jobs/sponsors-seen-as-crucial-for-womens-career-advancement.html

Sandberg, Sheryl. *Lean In: Women, Work, and the Will to Lead*. New York: Knopf, 2013.

NETWORKING AND RELATIONSHIPS
http://www.forbes.com/sites/jeannemeister/2012/08/14/job-hopping-is-the-new-normal-for-millennials-three-ways-to-prevent-a-human-resource-nightmare/
http://www.forbes.com/sites/christinapark/2014/10/03/eight-ways-for-introverts-to-shine-at-work/

GOING FROM ENGINEER TO EXECUTIVE
http://plato.stanford.edu/entries/ethics-ancient/
Duhigg, Charles. *The Power of Habit: Why We Do What We Do in Life and Business*. New York: Random House, 2012.
http://www.forbes.com/sites/nolanfeeney/2013/06/11/twitter-disclaimers-views-my-own-retweets-not-endorsements-social-media-law/
http://usatoday30.usatoday.com/sports/story/2012-04-22/Pro-athletes-and-financial-trouble/54465664/1
http://www.businessinsider.com/jim-rohn-youre-the-average-of-the-five-people-you-spend-the-most-time-with-2012-7
http://www.theguardian.com/careers/careers-blog/why-hobby-give-edge-job-application
https://hbr.org/1995/09/the-power-of-talk-who-gets-heard-and-why

START YOUR OWN COMPANY
http://www.cbsnews.com/news/tax-deductions-for-freelancers-and-consultants/
http://www.nolo.com/legal-encyclopedia/limited-liability-protection-llcs-a-50-state-guide.html
http://www.businessnewsdaily.com/7429-best-tech-startup-advice.html
http://www.paulgraham.com/convince.html

BONUS CHAPTER FOR MEN: HOW TO BE AN ALLY AND HOW TO HELP
http://www.geekwire.com/2015/commentary-bring-binders-full-women-tech-must-get-page/
http://www.huffingtonpost.com/2015/04/09/childless-more-women-are-not-having-kids-says-census_n_7032258.html
http://www.nytimes.com/2015/07/31/upshot/millennial-men-find-work-and-family-hard-to-balance.html

<ABOUT THE AUTHOR>

TARAH WHEELER VAN VLACK (BA, MS) is co-founder and CEO of Fizzmint, an end-to-end employee-management company. She has led projects at Microsoft Game Studios (Halo and Lips for Xbox), architected systems at Silent Circle, and holds two Agile development certifications through the Scrum Alliance: Certified ScrumMaster (CSM) and Certified Scrum Developer (CSD). She founded Red Queen Technologies LLC (a web development company), the Women in Tech Council (a charity that helps increase the number of women speakers at tech events), and InfoSec Unlocked (an initiative to increase diversity in infosec conference speakers), and co-founded Hack the People Foundation (a nonprofit mentorship initiative focused on underprivileged people in technology). She acquired her startup funds by cleaning out poker rooms in the Northwest and Las Vegas. You can reach her on Twitter @tarah and at TheTarah.com.

<ABOUT THE CONTRIBUTORS>

ANGIE CHANG is co-founder of Women 2.0 and Bay Area Girl Geek Dinners, VP of Strategic Partnerships at Hackbright Academy, and a Silicon Valley power player.

KATIE CUNNINGHAM, tech author published by O'Reilly and Pearson and a Python Software Foundation fellow, literally wrote the book on web accessibility and is an internationally recognized Python developer, keynote speaker, and lecturer.

ESTHER DYSON is the founder of HICCup and its Way to Wellville project—a five-year initiative to produce health in five communities around the United States. The basic idea is to help the five communities surround people with a healthy environment, including good schools (and early childhood education), good food, prenatal care, mental and dental health services, and access to traditional health care, then measure the results—which should be good—and encourage everyone to steal your ideas!

KEREN ELAZARI is a GigaOM analyst, *WIRED* and *Scientific American* contributing author, former hacker, cyber security researcher, the first Israeli woman to speak at TED, and an internationally recognized security thought leader featured frequently in the media and global at security events.

MIAH JOHNSON, senior systems and operations engineer at Simple, has decades of Unix and Linux experience, is a transwoman and queer, and is the funniest nerd on Twitter.

KAMILAH TAYLOR, software engineer at LinkedIn, taught herself mobile on the job and has filed a patent. Previously at Wolfram Research, she has an MS in computer science and robotics from University of Illinois at Urbana-Champaign and a BS in math and computer science from the University of the West Indies at Mona, Jamaica.

KRISTIN TOTH SMITH was CEO of Code Fellows, has been an executive at Amazon and Zulily, advises many startups, holds several patents, and was a Tauber fellow with a BSE and MSE from the University of Michigan as well as an LGO fellow from MIT with an SM in engineering and an MBA from MIT Sloan.

BRIANNA WU, head of development at Giant Spacekat, has been called the "Games Boss" in the press worldwide for her unapologetic advocacy of women. When she's not making trouble, she loves running and racing motorcycles.

GET IT TOGETHER!

9 3 1 3 15 8
Send the full name of the final
remarkable woman to Tarah!